How to
Turbocharge
Your **BUSINESS**

How to TURBOCHARGE Your BUSINESS

Numerology as the Power Booster

DANIEL R. HARDT, J.D.

How to Turbocharge Your Business
Numerology As the Power Booster
Copyright © 2020 by Daniel R. Hardt J.D.

All rights reserved. No part of this publication may be reproduced, distributed, or transmitted in any form or by any means, including photocopying, recording, or other electronic or mechanical methods, without the prior written permission of the publisher or author, except in the case of brief quotations embodied in critical reviews and certain other noncommercial uses permitted by copyright law.

Although every precaution has been taken to verify the accuracy of the information contained herein, the author and publisher assume no responsibility for any errors or omissions. No liability is assumed for damages that may result from the use of information contained within.

Library of Congress Control Number: 2020906020
ISBN-13:   Paperback: 978-1-64749-096-6

Printed in the United States of America

GoToPublish LLC
1-888-337-1724
www.gotopublish.com
info@gotopublish.com

Contents

Acknowledgments xiii
Foreword xvii
Introduction xix
   What is Numerology? xx
   Why Use Numerology in Business? xx
   The Layout of this Book xx

Chapter 1   Numbers as Symbols 1
   Indicators of Meaning from the Shape 1
   Categories of Numbers in Numerology 2
      Interior Numbers 2
      Exterior Numbers 2
      Core Numbers 2
      Transcendent Numbers 2
      Master Numbers 2
      Karmic Numbers 3

Chapter 2   Establishing the Founding Date 5
   Determining the Founding Date 5
   The Cycles of Numerology 7
   Calculating the Yearly Cycles 8
      Finding the Personal Month 9
      Finding the Personal Day 9
      Universal Year, Month and Day 9
   The Importance of the Cycles 9

Chapter 3   Choosing a Business Name 11
   Preliminary Considerations in a Business Name 11
   Brainstorming a Name 12

Chapter 4   How to Set Up the Chart 13
      Locating the Forms and Supplements 14
   Calculating the Core Numbers 14
      Calculating the Exterior Core Numbers 14
      Calculating the Interior Core Numbers 14

Some Principles of Delineation (Reading the Numbers) 15
The Integrative Vision Number 15

Chapter 5 Legal Format 17
Legal Proviso 17
    Indicators From the Numbers 18
Putting It Together 19

Chapter 6 Purpose 21
Calculating the Life Path Number 21
Coordinating the Cycles 22
Desirable Life Path Numbers for Your Business 23
    Tips for Established Businesses 24
The Birth Day Number 24

Chapter 7 What Motivates Your Business 27

Chapter 8 Talents 31
Needed Talents for Each Expression Number 32

Chapter 9 First Impressions 33
Calculating the Personality Number 33
    Example of Element Coordination 34
    Hidden Desires 35
    Reading the Personality Number 35
A Quick Check for Building Immediate Rapport 35

Chapter 10 Action Method 37
Calculating the Integrative Vision Number 38
The Effect of the Integrative Vision Number 39

Chapter 11 Image 41
Creating the Image 41
    Developing the Image for This Example 44
    Image Statement for the Example Business: 44

Chapter 12 Preferences 47
Evaluating the Questions: 48

Chapter 13 Expansion 57
Motivation, Talents and Opportunity 58
Business Types by the Numbers 59

Chapter 14 Vision 61
The Vision Statement 61

The Mission Statement 62
The Business Plan 63

Chapter 15 Style 65
Business Address 65
    The Street Number 65
    The Street Name and Beyond 66
Telephone Numbers 66
    Effect of the Telephone Numbers 67
Work Space Environment 67
    The Styles for the Numbers 67

Chapter 16 Hiring 71
Preliminary Considerations 71
Specific Candidate Considerations 72
The Personal Year Cycle 72
Full Chart Comparisons 73

Chapter 17 Personnel 75
Number Characteristics that Apply to the Functions 75
    Business Functions 76
    Legal and Accounting 76
    Choosing an Attorney 77
    Choosing an Accountant 77
Business Functions 77
    Policy Making
    Management
Operational Functions 78
    Bookkeeping and Secretarial
    Marketing, Sales and Sales Management
    Production and Distribution of Products
    Public Relations
Promoting Staff 78
Caution 79

Chapter 18 Vendors 81
Considerations in Categorizing Vendors: 81
What to Look For in Vendors' Numbers 82

Chapter 19 Distributors 85
Categories of Distributors: 85
    A Joint Venture Partner 85
    Affiliates 86
    Retail Outlets 86
    Clickbank 86
    Craig's List and eBay 86

Chapter 20 Sales 89
Core Numbers in Sales 89
Integrative Vision Number
Life Path Number 90
Expression Number 91
Soul Urge 91
Personality 92
Birth Day 92
Best Approach to Customers 93
Vowel Approaches 93
Consonants Approaches 93

Chapter 21 Sales Management 95

Chapter 22 Clients 99
Customer Relations Approach for Each Number 100
An Example of How the Approach is Developed 101
My Thinking in Setting Up the Approach 102
The Final Statement of Approach 103

Chapter 23 Financial 105
Assessing Your Business Risk Comfort Level 105
Similar Number Groupings 105
Record Keeping 106
Long Term Financial Planning 107
For Long Term Planning 107

Chapter 24 Plan 109
The Elements of the Plan 109
The Business and Personal Charts 109
The Founding Date 110
Business Name 110
Legal Format 110
Purpose 110
Motivation 110
Needed Talents 110
First Impressions 110
Action Method 110
Business Image 110
Preferences 111
Planning for Expansion 111
Vision 111
Style 111
Hiring 111
Personnel Placement 111

- Vendors 111
- Distributors 111
- Sales 111
- Sales Management 112
- Clients 112
- Finances 112
- Steps to Create the Business Plan 112
- The Operation of the Business 113
  - Employee and Staff 113
  - Vendors and Distributors 113
  - Sales 113
  - Client and Customer Relations 113
  - Finances 113

Chapter 25 Case Study Part 1 115
- Specific Comparisons for the Example Business 116
  - Original Data: 116
  - Reincorporation Data 116
  - Evaluation of the Changes 116

Chapter 26 Case Study Part 2 119
- Preparing the Plan 119
  - Name Choice 119
  - Legal Format 120
  - Purpose 120
  - Motivation 120
  - First Impression 120
  - Advertising 120
  - Employees, Vendors and Distributors 120
  - Approach to Business 120
  - Obvious Traits 120
- Business Plan for Life Path Numerology Center, Inc. 120
  - Mission Statement 120
  - Vision Statement 121
  - Corporate History 121
  - Office and Style 121
  - Expansion 122
  - Marketing and Sales Plan 122
  - Business Division 122
  - Personal Growth Division 123
  - Professional Training Division 123

Afterword 125
- How to Use This Material 125
- Limitations of the Book 125
- Further Study Opportunities 126

Appendix A 127
    Calculation Sheet 127
    Calculation Sheet, Filled in Sample 128
Appendix B 129
    General Characteristics of the Numbers 129
Appendix C 133
    Aspects Chart 133
    Calculation Sheet 133

Dedicated to

To Timothy A. Phipps

My Strength and Encouragement

Acknowledgments

A special thanks to all my students over the past thirty years who have challenged me and encouraged me in ways that even they did not know. Without their input and sometimes disagreements this would have been a lesser book.

I appreciate those as well who have written reviews or provided face to face skepticism of the possibility that numerology could make a difference in business.

I also thank those who provided venues for my teaching and readings to hone my understanding of numerology, I love skeptics who are open-minded enough to explore the material.

I especially thank Justin Daufenbach for his willingness to share with me his unique insights, which opened my study to a higher level.

By the same author

A Cupful of Gems
Daily Numeroscopes
Contributor to Wake Up... Live the Life You Love series,
Living on Purpose
Business Building by the Numbers (On-line class)

Foreword

It was 15 years ago this spring when I was first introduced to a Numerology book that would change my life forever. I was looking for a way to better understand my Reiki clients. I wanted to understand why some of them chose to heal and why others chose to resist healing. A quick glance at their birth date taught me not only what their challenges were but also which universal cycles were affecting them at this time. Without my understanding of the power of Numerology, it would have taken me several conversations over several visits to extract this information!

My clients could not deny the accuracy of this information. Numerology provided me with a valuable tool which allowed me to stand out as someone who really understood them. I had an edge over other practitioners. I took the extra mile to not only explore their birth date but also to share their personal Numerology insights with them which ultimately helped them on their healing path.

I rapidly gained a keener interest in Numerology! I couldn't get enough! In 2003 there was limited information online about this fascinating subject. But lo and behold I stumbled upon Daniel Hardt's website! I was so delighted to see that there actually was someone who held the same passion (if not greater passion) for the subject of Numerology!

As I grew my business, I followed Daniel very closely. I naturally signed up for his brilliant Daily Numeroscopes! What a treat it was to receive them every morning. It was as though he was speaking directly to me. Clearly, Daniel understood his craft and shared it so eloquently with us all. He was a pivotal influence in my early years of study.

I found it fascinating that even though we were both passionate Numerologists, Daniel had found an amazing niche. He clearly understood the value of applying the principles of Numerology to business. There was nothing at all like this on the internet! Nothing in print! He was a pioneer and the Aries in me loves a pioneer!

As my business grew Daniel continued to follow the newsletters produced by my business partner and myself. He never hesitated to comment on an article I had written that may have inspired him in some way. Daniel Hardt commenting on my work?! What?! What an amazing compliment to be recognized by the master himself! I'm not sure if he ever knew how grateful I was for his feedback.

As my practice quickly grew, so did my questions! Daniel never hesitated to return my countless emails asking for his opinion on a challenge I may have faced with a client. His input was always spot on as to what I needed! Even though it was clear that our focus on how we used Numerology was quite different, he was always able to offer me objective insight. His open mind is beautiful. He has taught me so much about how to be flexible and adaptable in my application of this amazing metaphysical science.

I was one of Daniel's first students in his "Business Building By the Numbers Online Class." At a time when I could be easily overwhelmed by the steep learning curve numerology provides, Daniel's course provided me with great relief. His lessons arrived weekly allowing me the time to grasp the information. I am a life path number 7 so I tend to over think and over analyze everything! This course created an organized, step by step process which rolled out beautifully.

How wonderful to have this course compiled into one amazing place! Daniel's book "How To Turbo Charge Your Business" is an amazing legacy which will continue to inspire business owners to reach out to be the best versions of themselves for years to come.

Thank you, Daniel, for continuing to inspire me to be the best version of myself.

Ann Perry
Professional Numerologist
Nova Scotia, Canada

Introduction

Are you bold enough to gain the benefits of numerology in your business? Most of your colleagues will laugh at the idea, but you don't need to share your secret of success with the scoffers. When you begin to outstrip them they will want to know what you are doing.

Numerology is not a fly by night, *woo-woo* program. It has been proven through millennia of profitable use. Pythagoras, the Greek mathematician (c 600 B.C.) is often considered to be the father of *modern* numerology. Because he was rejected by his native culture, he established his school in what is now Italy just before the Roman Republic was established. His work was much in demand by the political, military and business leaders of his day to provide insights into the characteristics of their cohorts and adversaries. Pythagoras was able to show the most propitious times to go to battle or the best timing for a business to move forward. He could help the politicians find common ground. In this book you will see how these actions were accomplished. You will be able to use these same techniques to further your own business, Consistent image, coordinated by the numbers, is important both to your bottom line and how you feel about your business.

In this book you will learn how to set up and read your personal and business charts. You will clearly see the importance of coordinating your personal and business numbers to eliminate conflicts. If you and your business are on incompatible cycles, you will quickly experience burn-out. When you are constantly fighting your business you will lose the zest for it that is needed for success. Bringing your business into line with your personal numbers can help make it a well-oiled machine. Conflicting energies is like sand thrown into the gears.

This information is appropriate whether you are just beginning to think about a business or have been long established. You have an advantage if your business is still in the formative stages, because you can set it up from the start without needing to make desirable changes.

With numerology you can determine whether the business address and telephone number are conducive to success. You can choose appropriate colors to identify your business, and you can find the most comfortable style for your office. Some numbers lend themselves to a formal, elegant setting; others cry out for a casual look. Find out what your business numbers have to say.

Following the numbers is as important for an employee as for the business owner. If the employee's personal numbers do not match the numbers of the business you have a potentially unhappy employee that may unintentionally sabotage the company. Numerology can help you to make the best hiring decisions and take the guess work out of promotions.

Attorneys, salespeople and help desk personnel will find the Quick Check invaluable. With the Quick Check you can build immediate rapport with total strangers just from how they introduce themselves. Once you learn this technique, you will confidently connect with customers and clients. People will want to do business with you.

You will find a wealth of instruction in this book to make your work life more productive. We want to be your guide to a fulfilling career in business.

What is Numerology?

Numerology is a metaphysical science based upon physics and mathematics. It is calculably accurate. The art of numerology is in the expertise of the reader in interpreting the findings. Calculating and reading a chart is easily learned and requires neither psychic ability nor esoteric talents.

Why Use Numerology in Business?

The business uses of numerology will become clear as you proceed through the chapters of this book. Setting up your business according to the natural energies to which it is attuned assures a consistent structure upon which to build. An uncoordinated system may contain conflicts that will sap the energy out of your business and cause you to burn out. Inconsistencies will subconsciously come across to your customers or clients as doubt. You build immediate trust when your style, décor, business form and advertising are all consistent with the numbers.

It is not feasible here to go into the scientific basis of numerology. That is a detailed study in itself. Suffice it for now to be assured that it works and will work for your business. Businesses that use numerology have a decided edge. You will see this effect in future chapters.

The Layout of this Book

Creating your personal chart is vital as a base for determining the business chart. Your personal chart was set at birth and cannot be changed. Any later modifications, such as a name change, do not change the foundation energies. Your business chart must be coordinated to your personal energies to avoid unnecessary conflicts in the operation of your business. For this reason, start with your personal chart.

Your business chart is set up in the same manner as your personal chart. There are some significant considerations in the business chart that are not present in the personal chart. We will go into detail on determining the best name for your business and determining the appropriate start date. For a corporation the start date is the filing date. For an unincorporated business, the founding date is less clear.

This book discusses each of the important elements and shows the application to personal and business energies. Once the full business chart is established, the remaining chapters will apply numerology to various aspects of the business. It is not designed to be a thorough text on numerology. It deals with modifiers and peripheral numbers only as they impact the conduct of your business.

This book contains what you need to use numerology in your business. For further study, if you wish, I would recommend the 2 volume set by Matthew Goodwin, *Numerology: The*

Complete Guide. Unfortunately this work is out of print and may be difficult to grab hold of. A more concise treatment is *Numerology: Key to Your Inner Self* by Hans DeCoz.

These works, and any text on numerology, reflect the opinions and expertise of the authors. As a result, you will find disagreements. I have not yet found a text with which I agree in every detail. I would caution you not to consult several different books in the beginning stages. You will only become confused by the differences in interpretation. Get the basics down first before you expand your research.

CHAPTER 1

Numbers as Symbols

In Numerology, each number represents an energy that vibrates at a specific frequency in hertz. These energies shape the universe and everything in it, including earth's physical plane and all plant and animal life. You are uniquely connected to a specific energy flow both inside you and from the outside. Each of these vibrations also has an associated tone and color.

The meaning of the numbers stems from the rate of vibration, which gives each number its unique characteristics. By ancient convention the shape of each number provides a clue to its primary emphasis.

Indicators of Meaning from the Shape

| A straight vertical line indicates an initiator with innovative ideas.
__   A straight horizontal line indicates sensitivity and non-confrontation.
C   A curved line emphasizes communication.
/   An angled line shows both passive and active elements.
O   A complete circle represents completion and love.

The upper part of the number shows the connection to the higher realm or the inner self. The lower portion shows the connection to the physical plane.

1. An initiator.
2. A passive observer and negotiator. Communicates with inner self.
3. Communicates at all levels.
4. Independent worker, Provider and hard worker.
5. Communicator, maintains independence and escapes confrontation.
6. The essence of love and nurturing, Inner communication.
7. Deep thinker and analyzer, but witty and charming at times.
8. High level development. Master of the physical plane.
9. Idealist. Complete in self, but often reaches out to others.

Categories of Numbers in Numerology

Interior Numbers: Number combinations in your chart that are unique to you and are derived from your name. These energies are an integral part of you.

Exterior Numbers: Numbers in your chart that show the energies to which you likely respond from your environment. derived from your birth date. These energies are shared by many other people.

Core Numbers: The major numbers of the chart. The five core numbers are:

- Life Path number: Shows your life purpose, and the primary lesson to be learned.
- Expression Number: Shows specific talents and abilities that you brought into this lifetime to help fulfill your purpose.
- Soul Urge Number: Shows what truly motivates you, and the type of activities that will be rewarding to you.
- Personality Number: The face you present to the world. It can also can reveal a secret desire
- Birth Day Number: Shows some obvious traits shared by everyone with the same birth day number.

Transcendent Numbers: Numbers beyond the core that combine interior and exterior numbers.

- Integrative Vision Number: Shows your usual approach to activities and challenges.
- Maturity Number: Shows a new emphasis later in life, often brought about by a traumatic incident that results in a new evaluation of your path.

Master Numbers: Numbers in your chart that show a high level of development for the purpose of providing service to humanity.

Consideration for master level status reflects not only individual growth, but also shows the level of society in accepting these energies.

Until society reaches the level to benefit from the master level, these numbers will not rise to this higher status. At the present stage of development the numbers that have reached master status are:

- 11/2 The bringer of enlightenment
- 22/4 The master builder
- 33/6 The master teacher
- 44/8 The master leader.
- 44/8 has not yet reached full master status, but it is beginning to fill. Its full power can only become evident when society no longer needs a ruler instead of a leader. Were it to fill faster than society is prepared for, it would produce a tyrant.

Karmic Numbers: Karmic numbers are numbers in your chart that show out of balance energies. The generally accepted karmic numbers are:

- 19/1 Inability to observe how others perceive you.
- 13/4 Inability to follow through in a systematic and organized manner.
- 14/5 Tempted to excess in physical pleasures.
- 16/7 Lessons to be learned in relationships.

A karmic core number is a roadblock to the full use of your talents and abilities until it is brought into balance.

A karmic number as a modifier is a lesson to be learned. You will face recurring events requiring the use of that karmic number energy. Karmic modifiers are not as strong a block to your progress as a karmic core number.

Chapter 2

Establishing the Founding Date

Later chapters will take you through an explanation of the elements of the chart and show how they fit together. It is not possible to cover everything in one chapter. As a result, subsequent chapters may modify your thinking about your earlier work. For example, this chapter is about cycles that are based upon the founding date for the business chart or the birth date for the personal chart. In obtaining the right cycle, you may find in a subsequent chapter that you do not have the life path that you desire. Both are important. You will see how to coordinate the two elements in a later chapter.

It is much easier to initially set up the numbers of the business for best advantage than it is to tweak them after the business is established. Don't feel overwhelmed. Just follow each chapter as it comes and you will begin to see the patterns. A well-constructed chart is a beautiful piece of work, but there is no such thing as a perfect chart. Because of the intricate intermeshing of the chart numbers, when you tweak one element to get what you want, it may create discord in another element. The desired goal is to create the most workable chart for you and your business.

Determining the Founding Date

For your **personal chart**, the start date is your date of birth.

For **an incorporated business**, the founding date is the filing date on the legal papers establishing the business. The business could be in the form of a full corporation, a subchapter S corporation, an LLC or whatever other legal form is available in your country. Once the papers are filed, you have created a new legal entity with a definite start date. Just as with your birth date, this date cannot be changed for the life of the business. The only way to obtain a more desirable start date is to re-incorporate, which in effect closes out the business and sets up a new entity

> *When we established Life Path Numerology Center, Inc. the date chosen by the numbers was October 22, 1996. When the papers were presented for filing, the clerk said that they would be filed the next day. That Delay was*

unacceptable to us. Upon explaining the reason for needing that filing date, it was done on that day. Initially she could not understand what difference a single day would make. She did not realize that a next day filing would put the business on an incompatible cycle. The effect of the delay would have been to disadvantage the business from the start. You may need to use persuasion in order to get the appropriate filing.

The challenge is more difficult if you are mailing the papers rather than hand delivering them. The right date is important enough to take whatever effort is necessary. Because this date will affect the flow of the business for its life, to get an appropriate date could well be worth a trip to the filing office. In some jurisdictions, on-line filing is available. If you have set the filing date according to your own cycle and the papers get filed a day later than you had calculated, you will set up a conflicting cycle that will be a problem as long as you are in that business.

The simplest way to create a founding date that is on the same cycle as your personal cycle is to add together the digits of month and day of your birth, and reducing that total to a single digit (keep adding the result until you reach a single digit.) Then decide when you may desire to establish the business founding date. Take the month and add a day that will bring the reduced total to the same number as your birth month and day total.

Example: With a December 28, birth date: (12)3+(28)(10)1 = 3+1 = 4, your personal reduced total is 4

If you wish to found your business in March, you will need a day that reduces the total to 4. Your Choices would be March 1 (3+1=4), March 10 (3+1+0=4) or March 19 (3+1+9=13=4) In April, you would choose a 9 day (9, 18, 27),. and in May use 8, 17 or 26.) For a corporation be sure to choose a day when the filing office will be open.

For **an unincorporated business**, setting the founding date is less defined. A business usually does not suddenly appear in full form. You get an idea and toy with it, sometimes for years. You plan out how you are going to set it up. You gain the financing, either from an outside source, from friends and family or from your own resources. As the process unfolds, the business becomes more concrete. A number of important events take place before you are ready to open your doors or market your products or services.

Choose a significant event that gives you the cycle you desire. Some examples of choices may be: the date of opening a business checking account, the loan closing date for financing the business, the date you open the doors of a retail establishment, the date of a lease or purchase agreement, or the date of publishing a website. Once you select the founding date, establish it by declaring it as the founding date in the minutes of the business or in a business journal. Once that founding date is accepted it becomes set and cannot later be changed without disrupting the business.

If you later decide to incorporate the unincorporated business, you must close out the books and start fresh. At incorporation a new legal entity is created with a new founding date.

The contents of this chapter may seem to be deceptively simple. The calculations involved are minor compared to setting up the chart in Chapter 4.

The Cycles of Numerology

In the personal chart, the cycles are set at birth. You cannot change them. Based upon your birth date, you were born into one of nine cycles. You are in the same cycle as approximately 11% of the total world population, which means that the same type of happenings will occur to each person in your cycle at the same time. The specific events will differ, but they will be of the same nature. On an active business day, for example, everyone in that cycle will be set for an active business day. In a social day, everyone in that cycle will be more social. You have a natural affinity for people who are on your same cycle.

Each person will respond to that energy in an unique manner. Just as when the weather is hot, some people will cocoon in an air conditioned space, but others will be out in it at the beach, mowing the lawn or basking in the sun. Health factors, cultural preferences and other external influences will color the activities. So, even though millions of people are responding to the same energy, their days may be quite different in the specifics.

The personal year cycle is 9 years long. It follows a natural progression from 1 through 9. Everyone goes through the same 9 personal years, but at different times depending upon the date of birth. Some basics of each personal year are as follows:

1. PY = Fresh start. Take the initiative to bring something new into your life.
2. PY = Wait patiently for the seeds planted in the 1 year to sprout. Relax.
3. PY = Communicate and sell your plans and ideas. Enjoy the social life.
4. PY = Work hard to build a solid foundation. Take care of financial and legal matters
5. PY = You will be bombarded with new opportunities. Restlessness keeps you moving.
6. PY= Home and family emphasis. Connect with friends
7. PY = An introspective evaluation of where you are and where you are headed. You need time alone.
8. PY = A year of accomplishment. Peak talents and support occur. Don't waste a minute of this positive energy.
9. PY = Discard the junk and unnecessary remnants of past projects. Reach out to others. Prepare for a new phase of your life as you again move into a 1 PY.

As you can see from this quick overview, if you are in a 7 personal year, which is introspective, and your business were in an 8 personal year, which is full steam ahead, you would be in a constant quandary whether to take the time that you need for yourself to the detriment of the business, or charge forward for the sake of the business and frustrate your own needs. Neither choice is desirable. When you and your business are on incompatible cycles, you are never in sync. Every year is a new conflict. It is only a matter of time until you give up.

Adjacent cycles, such as the 7 and 8 or 3 and 4, etc., tend to be out of sync. Cycles that are 2 or more years apart have some years that are compatible and other years that may contain conflict.

> **Definitions**
>
> **Cycles** – a pattern of events that recur on a consistent basis, such as the seasons or the months of the calendar, or the time on a clock.
>
> **Energies** – the vibrational frequencies of the elements that shape the earth plane and all that is in it. Each vibration in hertz is designated by a symbolic number and a corresponding color and tone.
>
> **Personal Year (personal month, personal day)** – The designation of where you are in your birth cycle. The number of your personal year discloses the nature of the surrounding energy that has the strongest impact upon events during that year.
>
> **Universal Year (universal month, universal day)** – shows the nature of the energy influencing the broader society.

Calculating the Yearly Cycles

For your personal chart use your birth date; for a business, use the founding date. The current personal year is determined by adding together the numbers of the month and day and combining the result with the current year. This calculation will give the personal year number for this year. Numerologists are about equally divided over whether the personal year extends from January 1 through December 31, or if it extends from birthday to birthday. Based upon scientific research and client feedback over many years, I am convinced that following the calendar year is most accurate.

It is well to establish good practices from the beginning. Although some numerologists differ in their approach to the science, in this book, I would like you to use my methodology and nomenclature so that we are on the same page when questions arise.

For greater accuracy in obtaining karmic numbers and master numbers (See Chapter 1) add the digits of each segment of the date separately, then add the reduced number of each element for the final result. You will remember from the first chapter that reducing a number results from adding the digits of the number together until you get a single digit or a master number. In numerology calculations always use 4 digits for the year.

Examples:
To obtain the Universal Year, merely add together the digits of the current year. 2018 is 2+0+1+8 = 11 (a master number.) Because no one lives continuously on the master plane, we show both levels of the master numbers with this notation 11/2.
To obtain your personal year, add the month and day of birth to the current calendar year number.
A December 28, birthday would give a personal year of 6 for 2018
1+2=3   2+8=1   2+0+1+8=11/2; 3+1+11=(15)6

Since 2018 is 9 years later from 2009, you would be back in the 6 personal year. If a memorable event occurred or you have a journal to remind you of the events of 2009, you are now into that same energy at a higher level. You will experience events of a similar nature.
Notation memo: Master numbers are written 11/2, 22/4, 33/6, 44/8 Karmic numbers are written 19/1, 13/4, 14/5, 16/7.
All other double digit results are written (15)6, (17)8, etc.
Following this notation system helps to remind you when you are working with master or karmic numbers. Failure to use this system will not, however, cause errors in the results.

Finding the Personal Month
Add the calendar month number to your personal year number to find the personal month.

Finding the Personal Day
Add the calendar day number to the personal month number to find the personal day number.
Example: Finding personal month and personal day for July 17, 2018, in a 6 personal year.
6 {personal year) + 7 (July calendar month) = 13/4 (personal month)
4 (personal month) + (17) 8 =(12)3 (personal day)

Universal Year, Month and Day
To find the universal year simply add together the 4 digits of the current year.
To find the universal month add together the universal year number and the calendar month number.
To find the universal day add together the universal month number and the calendar day number
Example: Finding the universal year for 2018 =2+0+1+8 = 11/2
Finding the universal month and universal day for July 17, 2018 in a 2 universal year.
2 (universal year) + 7 (calendar month number) = 9 (universal month).
9 (universal month) + (17)8 (calendar day number) = (17)8 (personal day).

The Importance of the Cycles

The personal and universal year cycles are 9 years long. Each of us proceeds through the 9 years consecutively from 1 through 9, but we do not all proceed from the same base date, so we are not all on the same cycle.

The universal year shows the general tenor of society. This cycle affects the energies controlling the culture, politics and business. It impacts you from the outside.

Your personal year shows where you fit into the universal structure. You are born into this cycle and it cannot be changed.

If your personal year is the same as the universal year you will be in sync with society. The same type of events will be happening to you as are occurring throughout the culture. If your cycle is incompatible with the universal cycle, you will never truly be in tune with society.

Your business will bring you less conflict if the business cycle is the same as your personal cycle. If you and your business are in incompatible cycles, you will constantly fight it and burn out.

In a later chapter we will go more deeply into the compatible numbers.

CHAPTER 3

Choosing a Business Name

"What's in a name? That which we call a rose By any other name would smell as sweet."
Romeo and Juliet, Act II by William Shakespeare

The name of a person or an object carries with it a certain vibration. When that name is spoken, it emits the specific energy contained in its letters For example, Robert has a different energy from Bob; William differs energetically from Bill.

Choosing an appropriate business name is not an easy assignment, but it is worth spending whatever time is necessary to get it right. The success of your business could rest upon the name you select. It is that important. I don't want to cause you to freeze up for fear of making a wrong choice. Just follow through with the exercises and you will come out with a name that is just right for you.

Preliminary Considerations in a Business Name

The name must be broad enough to cover anticipated expansion. Too narrow a name will be limiting. For example, *Mary's knit booties* may be too narrow to allow expansion into scarves and sweaters.

Determine whether this name will be an umbrella name with other divisions under it or whether you intend to operate under a d/b/a (doing business as).

Find a name that is general enough to cover your anticipated activity, but is still descriptive of the nature of the business. Some major corporations have names that don't follow this rule. Their activities may be too far ranging to find a common element. When you get prominent enough that your name is a household word, it probably doesn't matter whether the name is descriptive. Xerox is an example of such a name. If you anticipate that your business will rise to this level, you can ignore this tip.

The name must be legally available. Whether or not you immediately incorporate, you will want a name that is not registered to another company. You can check availability with the office in your jurisdiction that handles incorporations. Do the check only when you have a name that you have decided to use.

Be careful of the length of the name. You will be writing it often.

The name should have marketing viability. Avoid clichéd terms or clever puns in the name. Avoid words that have societal connotations that could be misinterpreted or become outdated.

The form of the business (which will be discussed in the next chapter) need not be considered in choosing the name. Generally such additions as Inc, Ltd, GmbH, AG or Corp are not delineated (added into the calculation.) If the word "Company" or "Corporation" is an integral part of the name, you would add that word to the calculation. For example, Microsoft Corporation would delineate "Corporation".

Brainstorming a Name

In choosing a name, you want as many options as possible. I would recommend a brainstorming session either solo or with others interested in the business. Write down every name that may pertain to the business. Do this exercise without judgment or discussion. No name is too far out or inappropriate for this purpose. Get as many as you can on the list. Try for at least twenty. One hundred would be better. Let this be a free flowing, creative session. Chances are that you will come up with ideas that you would not have considered without this exercise. The name you ultimately choose could well be one that would not have come to mind without eliminating the judgment in advance.

Go through the list and cross off any names that are not suitable. Rank those that remain in order of your preference.

In the next chapter you will learn how to calculate the numbers for a name. Run the numbers for the top names. In future chapters we will coordinate these numbers with your personal chart and the start date.

If you already have an established business, evaluate its name and start date. Don't do anything yet to correct discordant energies. In later chapters you will be given some tweaks that will help smooth out the rough spots. In a few instances, the energies may be so discordant that the only solution is to close out the business or sell it. In these few cases you may already feel the burn-out or wonder why your progress has been stymied.

If you are considering the purchase of a business or a franchise, run the numbers of the business under consideration for a fit to your numbers. Even though the purchase may otherwise seem to be a good deal, if it is not harmonious with your energies, it is not a good deal for you.

CHAPTER 4

How to Set Up the Chart

Initially we will do a basic personal profile. The calculations are the same for an individual or a business. In later chapters we will consider various modifiers that provide important nuances.

> **Definitions**:
>
> A numerology **chart** is the calculation results
>
> A numerology **report** is a written explanation of the calculation results
>
> A numerology **reading** is an oral report

Data for the Chart

Personal:

    Full name at birth including first, middle(s) and last
    Date of birth in this format mm/dd/yyyy
    Name currently used

Business

    The full legal name of the business
    The founding date - Date of incorporation or the determined start of business

Create your personal chart first. You will need this data for later comparison with your business chart.

The basic chart contains the calculations of the core numbers. The core numbers are the life path, the expression, the soul urge, the personality and the birth day. Some numerologists use only four of these numbers. You will find these core numbers designated by different names in some of the books. In this book, for consistency, please follow along with our method and nomenclature to be sure that we are talking about the same numbers when you have questions.

Locating the Forms and Supplements

The **Calculation Sheet** is located in Appendix A. You may want to print out several copies.

You will also find a **filled in sample Calculation Sheet** (this is my personal chart. As you follow the chapters, you will know more about me from this chart than I may want you to know.)
The general meanings of the numbers: number meanings are in Appendix B.
The Aspects Chart is in Appendix C.

Calculating the Core Numbers

Numbers derived from the date of birth are exterior numbers and impact the entity from outside. Numbers derived from the name are interior numbers and show energies that are contained within the individual or business.

Calculating the Exterior Core Numbers

Using the calculation sheet, place the date of birth on the top line in the following format: mm dd yyyy. Always use the four digit year in your calculations.

In numerology, the term reducing the number means adding the digits together until a single digit or a master number is reached. Use the master number in your calculations, for example 11 instead of 2. The master numbers are 11, 22, 33 and perhaps 44. In the chart, designate the master numbers as 11/2, 22/4, 33/6, 44/8.

Reduce each of the elements of the birth date separately and place the reduced numbers or master number in the second line. Add the reduced or master number values together and continue to add the total until you get a single digit or a master number. This number is the life path number, the major exterior core number. It shows your life purpose and primary life lesson.

The second exterior core number is the day of birth. Deriving this number requires no calculation except to reduce double digit dates. It shows obvious traits that are shared by all entities with the same reduced birth day number. Example: 5, 14 and 23 = 5. Anyone sharing any of those birthdays would be seen as active, risk taking and easily bored.

Calculating the Interior Core Numbers

The first step is to convert the letters to numbers. In the Pythagorean System, which we use, the alphabet is laid out in rows 1 through 9 as follows:

This conversion table is for the English alphabet only.

1	2	3	4	5	6	7	8	9
A	B	C	D	E	F	G	H	I
J	K	L	M	N	O	P	Q	R
S	T	U	V	W	X	Y	Z	

We use Y and W sometimes as a vowel and sometimes as a consonant. If the Y or W follows another vowel and shares a sound with it, we consider it to be a vowel as in Ray or Rowe. If it has a separate sound it is a consonant, as in Young or Wade.

Print the full name (first, middle(s), last) of the person at birth on line #3. Use the name exactly as it appears on the birth certificate. If the certificate contains an error, it may still provide the most accurate result. Try running a chart as it should be and compare the two to see which fits you best. Designations such as Jr or Sr are not calculated. Use a hyphenated last name as a single name.

On line 2 place the value of each of the vowels above the vowel. On line 1, total the value of the vowels in each name separately. Place double or triple values in parentheses and place the reduced value outside the parentheses. Add the reduced value of the vowels from each of the names. This number is the soul urge. It shows the motivation, or what needs to be included in life for fulfillment. *Example of notation: (23)5.* See the sample calculation sheet in the appendix for the format.

Place the value of each consonant under the letter in line 4. On line 5 total the consonant values from each name as you did for the vowels. This number is the personality. It shows the first impression that strangers get. It is how you project yourself to the world.

Now, on line 6, for each name, add the full numbers from lines 1 and 5 (the numbers in parentheses) again place double or triple digit numbers in parentheses and place the reduced number outside. Total the reduced numbers across and continue to reduce the total until you reach a single digit or master number. See the sample calculation sheet for an example.

The core numbers derived from the name are:

- Soul Urge derived from the total of the vowels.
- Personality derived from the total of the consonants.
- Expression derived from the total of all the letters.

Some Principles of Delineation (Reading the Numbers)

Numbers derived from the whole are stronger than numbers derived from a part. (The life path is stronger than the birthday. The expression is stronger than the soul urge or personality.)

Vowels are stronger than consonants. (the soul urge is stronger than the personality)

Resolving number conflicts: the stronger number controls and the weaker number modifies it. Read the stronger number first.

The Integrative Vision Number

The integrative vision number transcends the interior and exterior numbers. It is derived by adding together the 5 core numbers and reducing (add together the digits until you reach a single digit or a master number) the total. The 5 core numbers in order of strength:

- Life Path, total of the birth date numbers.
- Expression, the total of all the letters in the name.
- Soul Urge, total of the vowels.
- Personality, total of the consonants.
- Birth Day, the day of birth.

The integrative Vision number shows the most effective approach to life and work. Based upon the rules of delineation, this number should arguably be stronger than any of the core numbers, as it is derived from the entire core, yet few numerologists are aware of its importance.

In these early chapters, so much of the information requires an understanding of other pieces to the chart before it begins to make sense. Don't despair if these first few chapters seem to be too sketchy to use in your business. The application requires a coordination of several elements. This synthesis cannot be done until all these basic elements are considered.

One of my challenges is to cover the material in the most effective order. This book is set up to give you the skeletal basics in the first few chapters. As the course progresses, you will see how it all fits together. Later chapters will put meat on these bones as you apply the knowledge to your own business. As an example of how it works, the prior chapter concerns the name of your business. Choosing the best name requires coordinating the business name with your personal chart and the personal charts of key players. In addition the appropriate name numbers must be coordinated with the founding date. My recommendation is to study each chapter as it comes. Understand the material and get a sense of that element. Know that if you follow through it will come together. Don't panic if you don't immediately see the full picture.

When you think that you already know the material, you tend to skim it and miss some of the important nuances. These chapters contain my views on certain elements, which may differ from other books. You will not find some of the material in any other available publications.

Using numerology is a step-by-step process. Setting up a chart, for example is basic whether for a personal chart or a business chart. The emphasis and interpretation will differ by the use. This book is designed to lead you through the steps to a full understanding.

CHAPTER 5

Legal Format

Legal Proviso

This chapter will not cover tax tips or business strategy. The purpose is to give the appropriate structure for the numbers of your chart. As you go through this material you may want to have your personal chart in front of you.

Whatever the format you determine, it is advisable to consult with an attorney and an accountant for the actual construction of the legal entity. There are many intricate details in setting up a business for which you will want competent help. This chapter deals solely with the format from a numbers viewpoint. It does not purport to give legal or accounting advice.

The legal format can include a sole proprietorship, a partnership or a corporation. This is too limited a designation. There are several hybrid or alternative structures that may be available. These possibilities could be different depending upon the country or jurisdiction. A corporation provides the possibility of limited personal liability and may be desirable no matter what style your business takes.

In order to gain the best structure for your particular business, several choices must be made. If you are a sole proprietor at heart, you may form a corporation that has a limited structure. In the United States, we have the possibility of a Subchapter S corporation which has some of the corporate benefits, but that is taxed on the personal return as an unincorporated business. A "C" corporation can be set up with either a minimal number of officers and board members or with a large organization. A Limited Liability Company (LLC) is another possibility with different parameters. This form is most suited to a professional practice.

If your numbers tend more strongly toward a partnership, you also have some choices. It can be a straight partnership with each partner participating to the extent provided for in the contract or it could be a limited partnership.

The legal format should be determined in consultation with appropriate professionals to be sure that your business is complying with local and national laws.

From the prior material you will remember that there are 5 core numbers. For the purpose of this chapter, pay particular attention to the life path number (reduced total of the start date), the expression number (reduced total of the name letters converted to numbers) and the soul urge (reduced total of the vowels).

Your personal chart is the starting place for your business numbers. You want the business numbers to be reasonably compatible with your personal numbers. To the extent possible avoid major conflicts in these primary positions. See the number summary below.

The business format must be one with which you are comfortable. Getting the business numbers to agree with your personal numbers will provide a smoother operation. Discordant numbers will create constant tension between you and the business. You probably will not get a final fix on your business numbers just with this chapter. For now, pay attention to how the desired numbers are determined. I know that you are impatient to put it all together and see the finished product. Be patient a bit longer. There are so many considerations that are based upon other pieces not yet covered.

Indicators From the Numbers

1- A strong 1 in your core indicates the ultimate entrepreneur. This number demands an innovative approach. The lesson of the 1 is to stand on your own two feet and create your own accomplishment.
2- This is a partnership number. The 2 prefers to work behind the scenes and make sure that all the details are completed. It is difficult for a 2 to do the necessary promotion to make a business succeed. The 2 will benefit by combining with a front person.
3- This number is a promoter and sales person. The 3 can be a spendthrift and often lacks business discipline. It is generally not a strong number standing alone in a separate business. The 3 often is highly successful with strong company backing. It is a desirable adjunct in the chart, but needs more sturdy numbers in key chart positions.
4- This number is a work horse. Because of the need for security that is built into this number, a 4 business person will prefer the protection of the corporate format. The business created by a 4 will be solid, but generally limited in scope. The 4 has difficulty delegating. He has very set ideas of how things should be done and an inner knowing of what will or will not work. This number works well for legal or real estate offices and related services. It is an excellent number for a manufacturing enterprise.
5- The 5 will probably not want the responsibility of a business. This number is somewhat similar to the 3. It can be scattered and easily bored. This number works well for party planners, cruise hosts, travel agents and import-export dealers.
6- The most balanced number. It can handle the full gamut of formats. The 6 energy is great for performers, care givers, teachers and any business dealing directly with the public.
7- The 7 will probably not be interested in operating a business. It is an analytical number that is great for research and analysis from a scientific laboratory to on the street surveys. It is intrigued by metaphysics, mathematics and the sciences. It needs financial backing so that money concerns do not interfere with the research.
8- This is the ultimate corporate CEO. If you are establishing the business, be sure that your planning in the long range is for strong growth. The corporate format with a substantial Board of Directors (perhaps even some outside directors) will bring this business to the top.

- 9- The 9 is a strong leader, particularly in humanitarian or environmental oriented businesses. Level-headed support is needed for this number to work in a business. The idealism and perfectionism of the 9 work from the heart, often ignoring sound business principles. Usually, the 9 functions best in a not-for-profit corporate setting. Without the discipline of a left brain board of directors, the 9 will likely give away too much and jeopardize the health of the business.
- 11- This number is a combination of the double 1 giving it the independence of an entrepreneur, but the reduced value of a 2, lending itself to a partnership. This is a high level number, with a mission to fulfill. It is a special category reserved for those who have reached a service level that transcends all the normal rules. This person needs to operate independently within a larger community.
- 22- This number requires grand thinking in a very structured setting. The full corporation is almost required. It will involve projects of too large a scale for an entrepreneur to carry out alone.
- 33- Another high service level. With the double 3 and the reduced 6, it is often working in conjunction with other organizations. Either the 33 business will be a separate corporation that works as an independent contractor or it will be an integral part of a business. A 33 business, like the 6, can be multifaceted and can handle the full choice of formats.

Putting It Together

Review the list of numbers above and see what your personal numbers show for your style of business. You will want to bring a compatible energy into your business. If you have chosen a name that gives you numbers in the main core that are opposed to your personal style, you should probably choose a different name. A name that you like that does not give you appropriate numbers can sometimes be tweaked to make it acceptable. A single letter change can create a different core.

If you are to be the primary manager of the business, you want the business name to be as compatible as possible to your personal energies. When others are involved, the final result must be compatible with them as well. Compromises may become necessary. If the personal numbers of the others are compatible with your personal numbers, a chart that works for you should also work for them. If you cannot find this type of coordination, reconsider whether you should be in business together. Fully understanding the conflicts could make it work, but why make success more difficult.

This problem often arises when a husband and wife decide to go into business together. By bringing the family ties into the mix, the challenge can become emotional. Some couples should not go into business together. Later chapters will cover these comparisons more fully.

Each lesson is bringing you closer to seeing the full picture presented by the numbers. So far, it may seem as though you are getting a bunch of meaningless, unrelated details. I know that can be frustrating, but hang in there. It will become clearer with each succeeding detail.

The most important activity in making numerology usable for you is to gain a thorough understanding of the nature of the energy designated by each number. When you are proficient in the meanings, everything else in numerology will fall into place. Merely reading through the meanings of the numbers probably won't do the job.

The better approach is to take the core numbers from your personal chart and learn those numbers well. It will be easier to relate to those numbers that are already an integral part of you. These are the numbers that are most important in setting up and running your business.

If you are already in an established business, do the chart for your business. Learn the numbers from the core of both your business and personal charts and see if there are major conflicts. Make this review now, but it is too early to consider any modifications.

Most charts contain number inconsistencies and even conflicts. You are not dealing with a single energy. As you work with the number meanings you will begin to see the conflicts within yourself. Later lessons will show how number conflicts can be used to strengthen your chart. Conflicts from your personal chart give you more choices of emphasis in your business chart.

When you have incompatible numbers within a single chart, you read the strongest number first and use the weaker number as a modifier. The order of strength in your core is as follows:

- Integrative vision number
- Life path
- Expression
- Soul urge
- Personality
- Birth day

Chapter 6

Purpose

This chapter and the next five chapters go into detail concerning the core numbers plus the integrative vision number. With this information you will be able to get closer to the desirable numbers for your chart.

Don't expect a perfect chart. That animal does not exist. You are trying for the most workable chart.

This Chapter considers the life path number, the strongest external number in the chart. It sets the purpose that the business is designed to fulfill. From the life path number, you will incorporate a major lesson and certain traits and abilities that become a base for moving forward.

Start with the strongest core numbers first, because they are the numbers that would cause the greatest conflicts if out of alignment with your personal numbers. The conflict is more easily overcome in less potent core numbers.

Some numerologists consider the life path number to be the strongest number in your chart. We would argue that the integrative vision number is stronger and the expression is equivalent. In any case, these numbers are all stronger than the soul urge, the personality and the birth day numbers.

Calculating the Life Path Number

By way of review, the life path number is derived from the date of birth. Take each part (month, day and year) separately and reduce the total to a single digit. Reduce the total to a single digit or a master number by adding together the digits.

Example: May 30, 1940, May=5, 30 = 3+0=3, 1940=1+9+4+0=14/5

The life path is 13/4, 5+3+5=13/4

Definitions

Life Path Number – sets the purpose for which the business was established. Discloses a major lesson to be learned through the business.

Birth day (founding day) as a core number, only the actual day of founding is included. It discloses some obvious traits that will be observed in the business

This number tells you the primary emphasis of the business. You can get a sense of this energy from the excerpts in *the Meaning of the Numbers* in the appendix.

Coordinating the Cycles

When you calculated your personal year number, you got a total for the month and day of birth. Follow the same procedure for the month and day of your business. When you add this total to the founding year, you obtain the life path number.

Example: A May 30, birthday gives a month and day total from your personal chart of 8 and the year 2018: 8 (month and day total). 2018=2+0+1+8=11/2. Remember when a master number (11, 22, 33, 44) is reached in a reduction, we add in the master value rather than the reduced value.

8 (reduced month and day total) +11/2 (reduced year total) =19/1 for the life path. If you calculate the 2 rather than the 11, the result would be (10)1 instead of 19. You would miss the karmic overtone in the life path. Although karmic numbers present a challenge, they also provide a stimulus. If you are unaware of the karma you will struggle with the blockage without a clear method of balancing the energy.

Assuming the month and day total of 8 in the example, to get this business on the same cycle as your personal cycle, choose a founding date by taking the month number you wish for the founding of the business and figuring the day number necessary for the reduced total to equal 8.

Example: September (a 9 month) could be filed on September 8, 17 or 26 October (a 10/1 month) could be filed on October 7, 16 or 25 November (an 11/2 month) could be filed on November 6, 15 or 24.

Eliminate weekends and holidays from your list. Public offices would be closed and the filing would be delayed.

All of these dates reduce to an 8 total, when you add the year, for 2018, the life path number for the example is 19/1. If you delay the filing until the next year, you keep the 8 total for the month and day and add the year 2019 to it. For each succeeding year it adds a number to the life path number. So in our example waiting to file until 2019, while keeping with your personal cycle will give an 11/2 business life path number.

Of course, you will use your own numbers in calculating your month and day total.

Review your personal life path number. You want the business life path number to be at least compatible. Check compatibility by reading the number of your personal life path number and the business life path number in the Aspects Chart in Appendix C. The following list gives a quick comparison:

1= Entrepreneur
2= Partnership
3= Sales
4= Reliable employee
5= wheeler-dealer

6= Service oriented
7= researcher
8= manager
9= philanthropist

You may decide to delay filing the incorporation until next year to get a more appropriate life path number, or you may sense an urgency to do it this year. If the month and day are the same total in both charts, each delayed year will add 1 to the life path number, giving an odd or even number in alternating years. Generally, but not always, odd numbers are more compatible with each other and even numbers are more compatible with other even numbers.

In some instances, it will not be possible within a reasonable number of years to get a desirable life path number. In those few situations, you may choose to go with a different, but compatible personal year cycle. This is not the optimum arrangement, but as mentioned before, you cannot expect a perfect chart. There are too many interdependent variables.

Desirable Life Path Numbers for Your Business

The business life path number sets the purpose of the business. It influences your mission statement. It determines the primary lesson to be learned through this business. Because an 8 is often considered to be a money number, many novices immediately strive for an 8 life path number on the assumption that the business would then be financially successful. If your personal numbers don't support an 8 orientation, it may instead bring you grief.

The business purpose can be challenging, but is a major factor in reaching success. The purpose of each life path number follows:

1= to operate independently with the least amount of outside help or interference possible, and to accomplish from this independent base by initiating innovative actions.
2= to learn to accomplish through negotiation and patience in a non-confrontational manner by paying attention to details.
3= to persuade with words and to attract good luck through expressing joy. A social approach to business.
4= to be organized and systematic and to accomplish in steady increments through solid systems and methods.
5= to take reasonable risks in trying new ideas. A cutting edge approach to business. Learn to use freedom responsibly without getting into a rut.
6= to be service oriented, particularly in working with individuals. Learn to discern what is within the parameters of your responsibility and what should be left to others. Handle your duty responsibly.
7= to learn to operate in a faith mode, knowing that what is needed will be available when it is needed. Not suitable for most commercial businesses.
8= to operate on a large scale, with elegant formality. Learn to master the art of bringing in money through methods of manifestation. Requires a disciplined approach.
9= to develop an appropriate philosophy of giving for the benefit of society. Learn to bring your ideals into reality.

How well does the business purpose match your personal purpose? You will be constantly frustrated if the life path number of your business is opposed to your personal life path. You will see the difference very clearly by reading adjacent numbers. For example the organized and systematic 4 life path is diametrically opposed to the free-wheeling, spur of the moment, risk taking 5. Can you imagine a person with a stolid 4 life path trying to operate a business with a 5 lesson. Every day would be a battle within him, leading to burn-out.

Tips for Established Businesses

If your business is already up and running, the base has been set either by a corporate filing or a significant event declared as the founding date. When you run the numbers, you may find conflicts between your personal chart and the business chart. Depending upon the nature of the conflict, all may not be lost. You may be able to tweak the differences by emphasizing certain aspects of each of the conflicting numbers. Most of the energies are multi-faceted. It is often possible to coordinate the numbers by choosing to develop the areas that match and to ignore, if possible, the points where they clash.

To work with conflicting numbers you can develop a bridge. Subtract the smaller of the two numbers from the larger and reduce the total to a single digit or master number. The resulting number shows the energy that will help to smooth out the conflict.

Example: 5 and 7 are opposite extremes in energy. The 5 wants to be out and about, trying everything he is big enough to do. The seven wants to hibernate and analyze the world. The bridge is 7-5=2. The 2 energy emphasizes tact and diplomacy. Negotiation will help to find common ground.

If the conflict is too great, you need to decide if understanding the nature of the conflict and the different ways each side must be handled will be sufficient to allow you to continue. If you are already weary of the struggle, you may be best served by closing out the business or selling it and reestablishing your business on a more compatible base. You cannot change your personal foundation, so it is the business that must be modified.

Don't be too quick to make drastic changes without fully exploring your options.

A thorough knowledge of the meaning of the numbers will provide a wider range of coordination. Learning the number meanings well is the first step to competency.

The Birth Day Number

When you have established the personal year and the life path to your best coordination, you will be left with a specific founding day. Although the founding day is a core number it is of lesser strength than the life path. To have a conflicting number in this position will be easier to overcome than in the stronger numbers.

The founding day number shows an obvious trait of the business that will be evident to most people. Of lesser significance during the early years of the business, it will also show how to develop the life path lesson during a major time in the life of the business.

Obvious Traits from the founding day:

1- a lot of activity.
2- a laid back homey atmosphere.
3- a chatty environment.

4- hard work and concentration.
5- an unsettled environment with a lot of moving about.
6- a feeling of competence with true caring.
7- an aloofness.
8- major projects in the works.
9- idealism and perfectionism. Some tension.

CHAPTER 7

What Motivates Your Business

In the prior chapter we discussed the life path number, which gives purpose to your business, and the founding day number, which shows some traits that will be obvious to your customers. This chapter and the following two chapters cover the interior core numbers – the soul urge, the expression and the personality. These are the interior core numbers derived from the business name.

As emphasized throughout this book, it is almost impossible to obtain the perfect number in each of these positions. That is why comparison of compatible and inharmonious numbers becomes so important. As was explained earlier, some number meanings can be compatible with certain aspects of even a discordant number. If you are bringing together inharmonious numbers, be sure that you understand in what areas they can work together.

Disharmony in the numbers is not necessarily a fatal flaw in the chart. Understanding that the disharmony exists and the nature of the disharmony will allow you to realize that you are dealing with opposite pulls – a yin-yang effect. Knowing this challenge, you can better deal with it. Because of the challenge of discordant numbers, to minimize the difficulty, we try to confine the conflict to the weaker core numbers. Again, the order of strength in the core numbers is: life path, expression, soul urge, personality and founding day.

Of course, in each of these comparisons, your personal chart is the reference. Ideally, the numbers should be harmonious within the business chart and between the business and personal chart. You probably have some disharmony within your own personal chart. By now, using the skills you have developed to work with that discord will show you how to work with unavoidable discord in the business chart.

With the details involved in creating your chart, you may be tempted to just forget it, choose a name and founding date and bear the consequences. I can fully understand the frustration as you work through the chart. Believe me when I tell you that all the effort you put into getting it right will pay off big time. Your frustration will be even greater trying to work with a business that fights you at every step.

Once you get your chart firmed up, you have a blueprint for operating the business efficiently and profitably. Although you could hire a numerologist to prepare your chart, learning numerology for yourself will pay dividends in unexpected areas.

Recommendation: For the next three chapters, choose a name that you think might be appropriate for your business. Do the calculations with this name and make the comparisons. Even if you later change the name, using an example name will help you to more clearly understand the concepts. If the chosen name is not suitable, you will be able to see why it does not fit and see also what tweaks can be made.

This chapter covers the soul urge. Following the calculation method from chapter 4, convert the letters to numbers by placing the value of the vowels above each vowel on the Calculation Sheet (see Chapter 4). Add the vowel values for each name separately and reduce double digit numbers to a single digit or a master number. I have not included the conversion table in this chapter because it is on the calculation sheet for easy reference.

The soul urge shows the motivation behind the business activities. In the personal chart, it refers to items that must be in your life to feel fulfilled. In the corporate chart, I like to refer to it as the corporate culture. This term applies to unincorporated businesses as well.

You have a bit more free play with this number in comparing your personal soul urge. You may want to return to this chapter after reviewing your preferences in Chapter 12. Your answers will determine what you determine you want in your business. Analyze your answers to be sure that they reflect your comfort level. For example, if you say that you prefer an elegant office, but you are truly a down home boy who likes to put your feet up on the desk, you will resent the restrictions of a formal number. On the other hand, if you tend to like a more formal environment, but you set up a casual soul urge number, you may be constantly irritated when the office is always messy.

This lesson will be a basis for your vision statement and mission statement, which will be covered in more detail later.

In the soul urge you will sometimes come to a double digit number before you reduce it to a single digit or master number. Each of these double digits will give a slightly different feeling, but the general impact will be the same. For example 18, 27, and 45 all reduce to 9, and share the major essence of the 9 energy. However, 18 derived from 1 and 8 lend a practical business orientation to the 9 energy. This combination is particularly suited to a management role in a not for profit corporation. 27 is derived from 2 and 7. This 9 will want to stay behind the scenes, providing analysis and negotiating services. 45 is derived from 4 and 5. It is a freewheeling promoter of causes, but based upon sound systems and organization.

Here is a quick listing of the soul urge numbers and the type of environment each generates

1- This is a creative entrepreneur. The comfortable environment is a top directed business. The decision making is in the *boss* with little input from the staff.
2- This is an environment of consensus. Confrontation is frowned upon and harmony is a prime value.
3- A lively workplace with a lot of discussion and even extraneous chatter. Everyone values the workplace friendships from the top down.
4- A hard working, no-nonsense approach to business. It creates a rather rigid workplace with attention to detail and responsibility.
5- A party atmosphere. New ideas are encouraged. "Let's try it," could be the motto.
6- A balance between business practices and caring. The atmosphere is like family.

7- A think tank mentality. Ideas and philosophies are studied and discussed, with some question as to how much work gets done.
8- The emphasis is upon money and accomplishment. It requires maintaining an image of success. Major projects take priority.
9- A socially responsible company, conscious of environmental projects or philanthropic activities.

Much of the value of this chapter is in becoming familiar with the number meanings. By going through the suggested comparisons you will begin to see yourself more fully in some of the number descriptions. Those numbers that give an environment that you prefer would probably be desirable for the soul urge.

CHAPTER 8

Talents

Continuing the details of the core numbers, this chapter discusses the expression number, the strongest of the interior numbers. The expression describes what talents and abilities must be incorporated into the business for best results.

Numerologists do not agree on the nomenclature. Some numerologists call this number the destiny number. To avoid confusion I do not use this term. Some numerologists also call the life path number the destiny number. This discrepancy has nothing to do with the meaning and the emphasis of the expression. It is just different names for the same energy. The problem created by lack of standard terminology arises when I receive an e-mail of inquiry from someone who states that her destiny number is (whatever.) I cannot respond to the question because I am unclear whether the reference is to the expression or to the life path. That is why, early on, I asked you to use my terminology so that we can communicate.

Ideally you want the business expression number to be the same as yours or one that is compatible. Although this number is stronger than the soul urge discussed in the previous chapter, the expression has the possibility of supplementation through employees and independent contractors. So, if you are lacking some of the necessary talents, you may find a match with someone who carries these traits.

You still want to be careful that the expression number is not totally foreign to your own chart. If you are relying on other people because you lack the abilities needed, you will soon begin to feel incompetent in your own business. There will be times when you will need to step into the gap yourself. You will not be as strong a manager if you do not share at least the basic managerial talents.

The expression number is the sum of the values of all the letters in the name. To be sure that you are not deriving master numbers or karmic numbers inappropriately, follow the calculation instructions for setting up the chart (Chapter 4.) On the calculation sheet, place the numerical value of each vowel above the name and the values of the consonants below the name. Add together the vowel values of each name separately. Reduce double digits and add across to get the soul urge (vowels) and personality (consonants.) Next, add the double digit numbers of the vowels and the consonants for each name separately. Place the unreduced total for each name on line 6. Reduce the total for each name. Add the reduced totals to get the expression.

Needed Talents for Each Expression Number

1. Innovative ideas, independent action, not intimidated, a pioneer, apply ideas in a novel way.
2. Diplomatic, negotiating skills, attentive to detail, traditional, fine-tuned systems, harmonious atmosphere
3. Social atmosphere, communicative, salesperson, joyful approach, trust intuition and emotion more than facts and figures, spendthrift tendencies.
4. Organized. Create systems, solid financial base, methodical working, frugal.
5. Opportunity seeker, frequent changes in the business, risk taker, wheeler-dealer.
6. Relaxed business atmosphere, balance between strict business methods and caring, family-like relationships with employees, tasteful décor.
7. Analytical, not money oriented, researcher, no-nonsense atmosphere, problem solving abilities.
8. Strict management, good business acumen, elegant surroundings, traditional, money oriented ambition.
9. Emotional environment, philanthropist, willing to give a second chance, not a good judge of character.
11- Thinker, intuitive business person, needs faith.
22- Must think on a grand scale, major projects of lasting importance.
33- Teacher, Preserver of knowledge.

As you go through the numbers of your personal chart and the potential business chart, reading the meanings of the numbers will give you a better idea of what is required from the expression number.

Are you beginning to see the interplay of the numbers within a chart and between the charts? Don't be too concerned if the ideas are still a bit muddy. Clarity will come as you continue to work with the numbers. Again there is nothing more productive in numerology than gaining a full understanding of the nature of the energies designated by each number. It may seem discouraging at first, but before long, the numbers will seem to just fall into place. When you experience that clarity everything else in numerology will come together. For some people this clarity is a gradual process, for others it can be sudden, almost as an epiphany.

Chapter 9

First Impressions

This lesson covers the last of the core numbers in your business chart. By this time, if you have been following the material with a specific business name and start date, you have a better idea of how the chart describes the business. A later lesson will offer a clearer picture of the necessary co-ordinations between the personal chart and the business chart.

At this point, begin to analyze your personal chart and compare it with your business chart. You will find numbers that create a less than desirable match. You may be ready to do some tweaking on your own. Simply by changing a single letter of the name you will get a significant change in the chart. If you can determine what numbers might be an acceptable target to shoot for, you can more easily find modifications to get to that number.

Remember, except for the personal year cycle, the goal is not necessarily to achieve the same number as your personal chart, but it should be a number that is not in conflict. If you have another person who is significant in the business and who will be involved in the day to day operation, run that person's chart as well. As I mentioned in a previous lesson, key players should have charts reasonably compatible with your own, although they can supplement some of your gaps. In some instances conflicting core numbers between the two of you can be made compatible by a business number that is different from either and compatible with both or is a bridge number.

For example: If you have an 8 soul urge and your cohort has a 3 soul urge, you both may be comfortable with a 6 soul urge for the business. The 6 has the emotional aspects of the 3 and the business acumen of the 8.

Calculating the Personality Number

The personality number is the total of the consonants in the name. To calculate this number, place the number values of each consonant beneath the letter. Add those values separately for each name and reduce the total (add the digits of the total until you reach a single digit or master number) Add together the reduced numbers from each name. Reduce this total for the personality number.

Example: *John Jacob Astor*
1 85/1 3 2/ 12 9
14/5   6   (12)3 = 5+6+3 = 14/5
John Jacob Astor had a 14/5 personality.

Notice in the example that I designated the total with parentheses unless it was a karmic number (karmic numbers are 19/1, 13/4, 14/5 and 16/7). Master numbers are also marked with a slash. The master numbers are 11/2, 22/4, 33/6 and probably 44/8. 44 has not completely filled to master level status, because society has not yet developed to the point of fully supporting it.

The personality number shows how people who are not familiar with a person or a business instinctively see it. This view may not be a true picture of the business, but it is how the business is presenting itself. If the personality number relates to the rest of the core harmoniously, it is likely to be accurate. If the personality number is out of sync with the rest of the core, it is a façade that will dissipate upon familiarity with the business.

Reviewing some of the **principles of delineation** (the art of reading a chart) remember that a number derived from the whole is stronger than a number derived from a part and that vowels are stronger than consonants.

Based upon these principles, the personality number is a weak core number. It is derived from only a part of the name and it is derived only from the consonants. Therefore when reading the chart, the other core numbers would be read first and modified by the personality number.

Example of Element Coordination

Using the example of John Jacob Astor from above: He had a (20)2 soul urge and a 7 expression. In this case, the soul urge and expression are both solid, detail oriented numbers. The 14/5 personality is not in sync with those numbers. Therefore, this man was showing a façade to the world.

> *John Jacob Astor was a man who thought deeply and analyzed everything. Nothing escaped his attention, but he didn't always share his thinking with others (his 7 expression). He was motivated to pay attention to the least detail in his business dealings. He was a good negotiator, and was not above manipulating other people to get what he wanted (his 2 soul urge). He showed himself as a risk taker who was open to unusual business propositions. He did not appear to want the facts and figures and appeared to make decisions on a whim. Other people were fooled into thinking they could put something over on him because he seemed to skim the surface of any presentation (his 14/5 personality). He could maintain the façade because of his quick mind. He grasped the essence of the plan as it was being presented, but kept his thoughts to himself until the appropriate time to announce a decision.*

A façade in the personality number is not necessarily a negative. It is an integral part of the chart and should be used appropriately to further your business ends. It may add a touch of an energy otherwise lacking to soften the severity of other numbers. In the example, the 14/5 added a sparkle in conversation to what would have otherwise been a heavy chart.

Hidden Desires

The personality number also reveals a hidden desire. If the personality number is coordinated with the rest of the core, there is a good likelihood that the hidden desire will be fulfilled. If it is out of sync with the rest of the core, that hidden desire is likely to remain a secret fantasy.

Reading the Personality Number

If your personality number is:

1. You want to be considered independent in your actions, a successful entrepreneur.
   Hidden Desire – to create your own business.
2. You want to be considered to be a negotiator and a peacemaker.
   Hidden Desire – to be an outstanding musician.
3. You want to be considered a good speaker or writer.
   Hidden Desire - to be the life of the party.
4. You want to be considered to be a hard worker and a good provider.
   Hidden Desire – to be a real estate tycoon or lawyer
5. You want to be considered to be on the cutting edge and up to date on the latest gadgets.
   Hidden Desire - to be a world traveling jet-setter.
6. You want to be considered to be a responsible family person and a caring individual.
   Hidden desire – to be a great actor or singer.
7. You want to be considered to be a person of intellectual depth and a good problem solver.
   Hidden Desire – to win a Nobel Prize for a scientific breakthrough.
8. You want to be considered a great leader in the business world.
   Hidden Desire - to be the CEO of a large corporation.
9. You want to be seen as a socially responsible person, who is generous and considerate.
   Hidden Desire – to change the world.

A Quick Check for Building Immediate Rapport

Another first impression from the numbers is the quick check. When you meet people for the first time, pay attention to how they introduce themselves. It does not matter whether it is a proper name, an abbreviation of the name or a nickname. The introduction is a clue as to how that person wishes to be perceived. It may or may not agree with who they really are as shown in their core numbers. By relating to the desired perception you gain favor with that person.

Over a lifetime, many people will take on a different name as they grow and develop. Nicknames come and go. When someone tries to pin a nickname on you or you decide to use one, it will stick if it relates to your core. If it does not fit your core, it will soon dissipate no matter how much you try to use it.

For the quick check use only the first name. If someone is introduced as John Smith, use only John. If he is introduced as Mr. Smith, assume that he prefers the formal presentation and use the last name. If someone is introduced as Mr. John Smith, than you are back to only the first name.

For the quick check, take the first vowel (remember, vowels are stronger than consonants) and determine its number value. The vowel values are: a = 1, e = 5, i = 9, o = 6, u = 3, w = 5, y = 7. Remember that y and w are used as a vowel only if they follow another vowel and share a single sound with that vowel as in Ray or Howard, or is the only vowel in the syllable. When two vowels together form a single sound, as in Laura or Keith, a diphthong is created, requiring reading the energy of both vowels.

If the first vowel starts a name, as in Amy, read only the vowel. If there is a consonant in front of the vowel, then read the first consonant as a modifier of the vowel. Use only the first consonant even if there are two or more consonants preceding the first vowel, as in Steve.

Examples:

Mary (also Daniel, David, Martin, etc.): first vowel = a = 1. First consonant = m or D=4

Mary will want you to respect her independence and unique ideas. If you want her to accept your proposal, you will need to find a presentation that makes her think it was her idea (from the a). Then you need to present facts and figures showing why it is a good idea while still letting her think it was her idea (from the m).

John (also Sonny, Joanne, etc.): first vowel is o = 6. First consonants j or s = 1. Approach John with an emotional appeal, perhaps related to home and family, or emphasize how the idea will bring benefit to people (from the o), then show him how he could take that idea and make it his own by adding his own spin to it. Joanne works here because the a of -anne is a second syllable. Joan would create a diphthong and have a slightly different variation.

Joan: Vowels are o = 6 and a = 1. First consonant is j = 1. From the o we know that Joan is well aware of her family responsibilities, but from the a we know that she values her independence. With the added j we can sense that she may feel like a martyr if the family demands become too heavy. Therefore, in approaching her, we would be careful not to dwell on the family needs. We may try to help her with creative ways to find a balance.

This process is particularly valuable for sales people, trial lawyers, complaint desk personnel and any business or profession that needs to persuade the public. You will find it helpful in all your relationships as well.

Chapter 10

Action Method

This Chapter covers the integrative vision number. It shows the most effective method of accomplishing the work of the business.

You will not find the integrative vision number in another text. Although some of the authors have hinted at this information, none have included it as a part of the chart. The integrative vision number is not a core number, but it can be argued that it is the most important number in your chart.

You may recall that one of the principles of delineation (reading a chart) is that numbers derived from the whole are stronger than numbers derived from a part. The integrative vision number is derived from the total of all the core numbers, and therefore is stronger than any of the core numbers. It also supersedes the concept of interior and exterior numbers (another idea that you will not find in the texts.)

The integrative vision number adds a dimension to the chart that addresses some gaps that otherwise are found in some charts. We have several examples within our own board members.

The chart of one Board Member is filled with 5 and 7 energy. These numbers are adequate for a teacher, but would not show the passion which she brought to her profession. Her integrative vision number is 33/6, the master teacher. By using the integrative vision number, her love of teaching is clearly revealed. Without this added information, it would have appeared that she was not truly in sync with her chart.

Another Board Member has predominant 7 and 9 energy. This member exhibited a restlessness and desire for change usually characteristic of 5 energy. This trait was very pronounced, but there was no 5 in his core. Knowing that his integrative vision number was a 5 put his need for change into proper perspective.

My chart is a bit different. I have a 9 soul urge, yet the 9 energy seemed stronger than the soul urge would indicate. When I found that my integrative vision number was also a 9, it made sense that I was often working from the 9 instead of some of the stronger core numbers.

Calculating the Integrative Vision Number

The integrative vision number is calculated by adding together the reduced numbers of all 5 of the core numbers and reducing the total to a single digit or a master number. This number is a significant determinant of how you approach life. It sets the default mode.

The core numbers are:

1. life path – the total of the full birth date.
2. Birthday – reduced number of the day of birth only.
3. Expression – the total of the number values of all the letters in the full name at birth.
4. Soul urge – the number value of the vowels in the birth name.
5. Personality – the number values of the consonants in the birth name.

The integrative vision number is the reason that we insist upon 5 core numbers. Using only 4, as suggested in some of the texts does not give the appropriate total. The texts that we recommend for our classes are Matthew Goodwin's 2 volume set, *Numerology: The Complete Guide*, which is now out of print and hard to find, and *Numerology: Key to the Inner Self* by Hans DeCoz, which is available through Amazon and other distributors. We recommend these texts because, for the most part, they accurately present numerology in a straightforward manner. If you are looking to the books, you will likely find disagreements with every author on some points. This does not negate the science. We all have much yet to learn. As we grope our way to a full understanding, we may take different viewpoints.

Matthew Goodwin does not give much consideration to the personality number. It almost disappears form his charts. Hans DeCoz does not consider the birth day to be a core number, and neither of them includes the integrative vision number. As a test, I have tried to delineate a valid integrative vision number that excludes either the birth day or the personality number. The results are meaningless to the approach.

In a business chart, the integrative vision number will tell you the most productive approach to your business. It may indicate a form of action that is not in keeping with the rest of the chart, and yet can be integrated into the core energies in a vital dynamic. The integrative vision number has nothing to do with talents, motivation or purpose. It is superimposed upon the chart.

Although the integrative vision number affects every aspect of the business, it is a number that should be allowed to express without tweaking the chart for a specific number. The operation of the core numbers will be the essence of the business. The integrative vision number is the result. When you have a workable core, the Integrative vision number brings in an energy that makes it all come together. However, you will want to check that the approach of the integrative vision number is not pushing you in a direction that is opposed to your personal integrative number. For example, if your personal integrative vision number is a 2 and the business is a 5, you will be uncomfortable with the perceived chaos in the business, but with your 2 personal Integrative Vision number, you may be too reluctant to venture. The business 5 integrative vision number will get you out of your comfort zone to help prevent stagnation.

The Effect of the Integrative Vision Number

A listing of the integrative vision numbers follows:

1- This number requires the business to initiate action. With a 1, creative ideas need to have free play.
2- This number suggests that negotiation will work better than confrontation. A traditional approach is indicated.
3- Communication is the key to effective action. Rather than a terse business conversation, there needs to be room for some social chit-chat.
4- Diligent work without much interference is best. Pay attention to the fine print and be sure that all details are understood and covered.
5- Keep a free-wheeling atmosphere. Sudden changes can be beneficial.
6- An harmonious family feeling should be maintained. Genuine caring supersedes business for business' sake.
7- Everything must be analyzed and thought through. Frivolity is not favored, although laughter and joking can relieve the serious overtone.
8- Keep a demanding workplace, but be sure that all your dealings are fair. Highest business principles should be enforced.
9- Perfection is desired, but there is room for a second chance. Reach out to the community in a spirit of sharing.
11- All actions of the company should relate to a higher purpose. An understanding of how the business enriches the lives of employees and customers will show this to be an enlightened approach.
22- The business must have a grand design. Building toward fulfillment of the plan will keep the work on track, provided that the goal is large enough.
33- a teaching element is implied in every activity. The work goes smoothly when adequate instruction has been given.

CHAPTER 11

Image

This chapter looks at the complete core chart and pulls from it the pattern that will sustain a consistent image for your business. Most likely, your chart has a variety of numbers from which to work. Some of these numbers complement each other, while others may be in conflict. You will be given the guidelines to make sense of the combinations.

You will begin to *see* your business unfolding as you balance the elements. By doing the explanation in a piecemeal fashion, the total picture may not have yet become clear. In considering each of the core numbers separately you received a fragmented view of the chart. In order to understand each element, this singular approach was necessary.

With this chapter we begin to look at the chart as a whole. Up to now, we have taken a picture of a business and examined the individual parts up close. Now it is desirable to step back and look at the whole business. Each of the parts becomes integrated into the total look of the business.

The image of the business goes beyond the physical look and feel of the facility. It includes many elements which are not always consciously evident. The business has a subtle aura that customers and vendors pick up at a subconscious level. It is this aura that helps a person to choose to become a customer. Customers will be attracted or repelled, depending upon their trust in the business.

With the numbers, you can control that aura. Instant rapport is established when everything in the business is supported by the energies shown by the numbers. A projected image that is inconsistent with the numbers creates an immediate distrust.

Creating the Image

The personality number shows the first impression of people unfamiliar with the business. The founding day number shows an obvious trait that will be immediately visible. These two numbers are the weakest of the core numbers and, although obvious in their traits, are of lesser importance in the overall image than the other core numbers. They will need consideration in the final result, but can be ignored for the moment.

For this lesson, the strength of the numbers is more important than the position. For example, the life path number tells the business purpose, but for the image we only consider that the life path is the strongest of the exterior number (numbers derived from the founding date). Since the expression is the strongest of the interior numbers (numbers derived from the name), these two numbers are the starting point for the image.

Step #1. Check the Aspects Chart in Appendix C to determine whether these numbers are harmonious or discordant.

Step #2. Most numbers have a fairly wide range of meanings. Look at the Meaning of the Numbers Chart in Appendix B. Make a list of the characteristics of each of the numbers of the life path, the expression and the soul urge. There are two main reasons to suggest the list: 1) writing out the lists impresses the number meanings in your mind. It is a simple way to become more proficient with using the numbers. 2) It is easier to make comparisons from lists. Pull out those meanings that the two numbers have in common. The wording may not be exact, but if the words are similar, add them to the image.

When you first begin working with the numbers, finding the correlations will be challenging. When you really know the number meanings, you will form a clear image immediately. At this stage there is no substitute for writing out the meanings. On those numbers that seem to elude you, try writing the list several times. The physical act of putting pen to paper ingrains the meanings more fully.

See my list below

Example: With a life Path number of 4, an expression of 1 and a soul urge of 9, my lists are as follows:

4	1	9
Practical	Born leader	Humanitarian
Down to earth	Erratic	Philanthropic
Underlying compassion	Innovative ideas	Change the world
Reliable	Own boss	Creative
Methodical	Own business	Artistic
Systematic	Pioneer	Perfectionist
Responsible	Strong Personality	Often used by others
Stable	Not easily Intimidated	Moody
Secure	Gains information for specific use	Arrogant
Conservative	Dominating	Compassionate
Not creative	Egotistical	Works with groups
Detailed	Risk taker	Attracts money
Too serious	Drive and determination	Charming
Trustworthy	New approaches	Well-liked
Moralistic	Honest Loyal	Charismatic
Honest	Reliable Starter, not finisher	Intuitive
Strong likes and dislikes	Dislikes routine	Dramatic
Survivor		Emotional
Good provider		Expresses feelings
Family emphasis		Fascinated by people
Shrewd		People attracted or repulsed
Often tactful		Not good judge of character
Narrowly focused		Often misreads others
Loves nature		
Manual worker		
Frugal		

In this example 4 and 1 are harmonious. 9 is discordant to both the 4 and 1. We would expect that the lists from the life path and the expression will have more characteristics in common and that the 9 list would contain traits that are different.

Step #3. Mentally absorb the lists until you get a clear picture of that energy. As you do this with each list you will begin to *see* that number. Start with combining the life path and the expression numbers. Look for similarities between their traits. Those characteristics that are similar in both lists are the ones to add to your image.

Developing the Image for This Example

Some of my thought processes:

Starting with the 4 life path, the image is one of stability, detail and hard work. The business must be financially sound, with precise systems in place. Money comes in steady increments. The rules of conduct would be well defined and put into written form.

Adding the 1 expression gives some breathing room to allow leeway in the enforcement of the rules. Although there is an underlying rigidity in the operation, new ideas, even cutting edge concepts will be considered. Reliability and customer loyalty are strong values. The 1 pushes for major accomplishment based upon innovative ideas.

The 9 soul urge, adds an emotional overtone to the atmosphere of the business. The perfectionism of the nine relates to the detailed systems of the 4. The business emphasis must include a value to society. If appropriate, some pro bono work would bring in money from unexpected sources.

The 4 and 1 are oriented to the business itself, without a lot of concern for a wider community impact. The 9 opens up a broader outreach.

This image statement will remain incomplete until adding your personal preferences from Chapter 12. You may pick up different traits or consider elements that I have excluded. There is no right or wrong image statement. Once you have developed the image for your business, it becomes a tool for the operation of the business and your interaction with customers and vendors. You should change it only if you find it inadequate for some areas covered by your business. Changing it on a whim diminishes the trust that a solid image conveys.

The image statement is a foundation for the business. It should be a reference for decision making, advertising and development of the business. By coordinating with the image statement, you assure consistency in your business upon which your employees, customers and vendors can rely. When the image is according to the numbers, it will ring true. Creating an image that goes against the numbers will create a discord that will be subtly picked up as false, and therefore, unreliable. That perception carries over to the business as a whole.

Image Statement for the Example Business:

There is a solid foundation of systems and procedures for the operation of the business, including financial record keeping and written rules of conduct. Employees are expected to be hard working and responsible with minimal supervision. Stability and mutual loyalty are expected from management and employees, and to customers and vendors. Attention to detail keeps the base intact.

The business builds upon this foundation through encouraging independent thinking and innovative ideas. When new projects are developed, they must be shown to be financially sound. The innovation must be supported by adequate data showing its feasibility. The business does not take untenable risks on the chance of a windfall profit. Risky speculative endeavors are not favored. It is honest in all its dealings, even if it seems that hype or exaggerated statements would bring immediate gain.

The business operates from a position of power based upon its integrity. Negotiations are tactful, but strong. Its position is well established by the detailed data at hand. The business does not take undue advantage of the other party through nondisclosures and ruses. Its dealings will be fair to all the involved parties.

The business is a responsible citizen. Its products and services will enhance society. Its operation will not cause harm to the environment. It will develop solid relationships by always giving full value for the cost. When appropriate, the business will be generous in donations to worthy causes, but not at the cost of its financial health. Pro bono work is encouraged when time allows. This philanthropic outreach will bring unexpected rewards from unusual sources.

Your image statement from the same lists may be different. Can you see how I have incorporated elements from the three lists to bring them together? When the life path and expression are in conflict, you may need to blend the elements or find a way to give each list its rightful weight. You may decide to go more strongly with one list for certain functions of the business and with the other in different areas. I can see this separation working when one list covers in house operations and the other list applies to customer and vendor contacts.

You may want to come back to this section after completing the preference analysis in the next chapter. You may decide to choose items for your image that match your preferences. Your preferences will most closely match your personal numbers, but you should also look at how they fit with the business numbers.

If you are having difficulty in finding the right blend, consider a bridge number. To find the bridge number, subtract the smaller of the two numbers you are comparing from the larger. Look at the traits of the resultant number to find elements that will bring the two together. In the example, the 9 soul urge is discordant. The bridge to the 4 life path is 5. That would indicate that the rigidity of the four needs a creative opening up to reach the idealism and emotion of the 9.

The bridge between the 1 expression and the 9 soul urge is 8, which indicates that to create a proper fit, the creative expression of the 9 needs to be well grounded, not whimsical.

The personality number shows the first impression of the business by strangers. As people get to know the business, they will see the true character behind that first glimpse. The personality number does not play a big part in the continuing image.

The birthday shows obvious traits, that is interesting to note, but just muddies the water if we try to incorporate it into the image.

The integrative vision number is how the business operates. It has less impact on the image than the three core numbers used for image determination. The integrative vision number provides guidance within the business, rather than in reaching out to the customer base.

CHAPTER 12

Preferences

This chapter adds depth to the image. A questionnaire is provided to help you evaluate the aspects of your business that fit you. Answer the questions thoughtfully and honestly. This exercise is best done in writing to be sure that you have clarity on each point. Taking time to fully consider each answer is time well spent. Do not answer as you think others may desire, nor according to some preconceived ideal in your mind. For example, if you truly do not mind stacks of paper on your desk, don't choose a neat, well-organized office because some guru has convinced you that a clear desk is necessary to success. Answer according to your usual or preferred style.

Thinking about your answers in advance will help you to better understand what you want in your work environment. Do the preferences from the viewpoint of your own business (boss) rather than from the position of an employee.

Being comfortable in your business is an important element of success. You will be in a constant battle if the business numbers demand a situation that is different from your preferences. In a conflict, most people will follow their personal preference over the preferences that suit the business. This choice often brings a subtle dissonance that your customers will sense as distrust.

Answering the questionnaire does not require any calculations. The application proceeds from an analysis of the numbers as they relate to your preferences. As you analyze the lists you will become better grounded in these meanings.

In your Image Statement you set out the meanings of the numbers of your business life path, expression and soul urge. These numbers may have been in harmony or they may have contained conflicts. In either case, you need to look at the energies of all three. Again, start with the life path number as the base; add the expression and then the soul urge lists in that order. The expression builds on the base if it is harmonious. If it is dissonant you will need to add elements from both, either blended or some from each list. The soul urge list modifies the other two.

Review your preferences list. On most of the answers you will not be at the extremes. When you are comparing your preferences to the numbers, there will be room for interpretation. Don't be as bound by the actual words in the lists as you are by the feeling you get from the lists. The primary situations to avoid are in those items where you have a very decided preference that goes against a strong opposite in one or all of your lists.

To make this lesson meaningful, I could find no better way than to go through the questionnaire item by item through each of the numbers. The most helpful part of the lesson will be in training you to be aware of the nuances contained within the numbers and to apply the general energy, even when it is not precisely stated. With master energy use the reduced number for this purpose; for 11 use the 2 list, for 22 use the 4 list, for 33 use the 6 list.

You may disagree with my evaluation. By making the lists you will gain insights into the nature of the numbers for yourself. Of course, for every list you will find exceptions. Conflicting numbers may push the preference toward the opposite end of the scale.

I have more fully discussed each of the numbers for the first 2 items to provide examples. For the succeeding items, I have used a simple description. This list is a guideline. You may be conditioned to certain practices by habit or exigencies of your business. Experiment with those areas where there is a discrepancy to see if tweaking the style would bring better results.

The questions show the extremes with the most rigid on the left and the flexible on the right. On most of the questions you will fall somewhere within the continuum. Using a scale of 1-10 with the left being 1 and the right being 10, write down for each question your best estimate of where you fall on the scale.

Evaluating the Questions:

1. **Do you prefer formal business attire or casual dress?** An additional consideration is what dress the type of business requires. Some occupations have a traditional uniform. Different numbers will show variance in how the same uniform is worn.

    - #1 –Quality casual or business dress with a twist The 1 is non-traditional and innovative, so we would not expect the dress to be too conservative. An added flair is appropriate. As a leader, the 1 does not go too far out of bounds.
    - #2 – Banker business suits. The 2 pays attention to detail and is traditional with an eye for beauty. We would expect the 2 to prefer suits and ties for a finished look. The 2 does not want to stand out, so will use earth tone colors with little adornment.
    - #3 - Casual. The 3 is happy-go-lucky, irresponsible and flamboyant. We would expect the 3 to dress according to the whim of the day, but probably to the casual side.
    - #4 – Suit and tie or quality casual. The 4 is conservative and stable. His dress would reflect the traditional values of a suit and tie style.
    - #5- All are appropriate.– with a 5 anything goes. With the love of the exotic, the dress could become flamboyant, but not consistent from day to day.
    - #6 – Suit and tie. Above all, the 6 dresses in good taste. With an emphasis on balance and harmony, we would expect traditional dress with an added flair, such as an unusual tie for men or a striking scarf for women.
    - #7 Casual to jeans and sport coat. The 7 looks good in anything he wears because of his fine carriage. Clothing will not be a main priority, so a causal or even disheveled

appearance is not out of bounds. He is too busy with inner thoughts to consider for long the outer look.
- #8 – Definitely suit and tie The 8 must always be dressed to the hilt with the finest quality suits. His dress is a statement of his accomplishment and a factor in his leadership style. Sloppiness is just not acceptable.
- #9 –Suit and tie for business, business casual with an arty twist. The 9 is artistic and dramatic. He is not likely to be too conservative, but his perfectionism demands that his dress be impeccable.

Example: From this list you can see that if you have a business with a 5 life path an 8 expression and a 6 soul urge, and your personal preference is casual, you will have difficulty in finding a comfortable compromise. The flamboyant 5 could give you the breathing room to be yourself, however, the 8 and the 6 would fight against it. If you can accept more formality in dress it can work, but you will lose any advantage of the numbers to insist upon jeans and a tee shirt. Check out your personal chart to see if your stated preference is really you.

2. **Do you prefer an elegant or casual office environment?**

- #1 – Ideas are more important than the environment to the 1. As a result, an elegant office is unlikely.
- #2 – The beauty, balance and proportion within the office are all important to the 2. It should be elegant with warmth. Every detail will be considered.
- #3 – the 3 encourages activity. Too much elegance is stifling. It should contain a dramatic flair, without too much emphasis upon tradition.
- #4 – The office of a 4 is above all practical. His frugality will make do with whatever is available without regard to coordinating the results. Embellishments will be minimal.
- # 5 – The 5 office will bring in an eclectic mix from the elegant to the gaudy, likely collected from world travels or other areas of experience.
- #6 – Elegance for the 6 comes from everything being in good taste. Balance, harmony and color are important. It exudes homey warmth.
- #7 – The 7 office will likely have books and magazines strewn about from pending projects. Décor is relatively unimportant.
- #8 – The 8 office is the showplace of elegance. It must be of the finest quality and with a traditional, cohesive theme.
- #9 - The perfectionism of the 9 would want everything in the office to be right, with a dramatic overtone. The 9 energy is artistic, so it would be somewhat non-traditional, but in good taste. Not ostentatious.

Example: With a 2 life path, a 6 expression and a 1 soul urge, good taste with harmony of color and proportion are essential to the 2 and 6. The 1 can be comfortable in the more traditional environment, even though personal preference would be more innovative. For this combination, I would start with a traditionally elegant office, then add some unexpected touches.

3. **Do you prefer a top down chain of command or group Consensus?**

    - #1 boss at the top who oversees everything.
    - #2 prefers consensus and committees.
    - #3 avoids rigid structure.
    - #4 definite hierarchy with defined chain of command.
    - #5 freewheeling with daily changes.
    - #6 chain of command, but with employee input.
    - #7 boss at the top.
    - #8 Chain of command with specific delegation of duties.
    - #9 group consensus.

4. **Do you prefer set hours or a flexible schedule?** Personal considerations may influence this choice.

    - #1 flexible schedule.
    - #2 set schedule.
    - #3 flexible hours.
    - #4 set schedule.
    - #5 flexible hours.
    - #6 could go either way.
    - #7 flexible hours.
    - #8 set schedule.
    - #9 could go either way.

5. **Do you prefer a set salary or money as it comes in?**

    - #1 as it comes in.
    - #2 set salary.
    - #3 as it comes in.
    - #4 set salary.
    - #5 as it comes in (or before it comes in).
    - #6 either way.
    - #7 set salary.
    - #8 set salary.
    - #9 could go either way, but probably should be a set salary.

6. **Do you prefer a home office or away from home?**

    - #1 away from home – needs to be with people.
    - #2 away from home needs a staff.
    - #3 away from home.
    - #4 home office. Works well alone.
    - #5 away from home and out and about.
    - #6 home office.
    - #7 either, depending upon the nature of the business.

- #8 away from home.
- #9 either depending upon the size of the operation.

7. **Do you prefer an urban setting or rural quiet?**

    - #1 urban setting.
    - #2 country quiet.
    - #3 urban setting.
    - #4 country setting.
    - #5 urban setting.
    - #6 either.
    - #7 either.
    - #8 urban setting.
    - #9 urban setting.

8. **Do you prefer working with a large staff or working alone?**

    - #1 work alone.
    - #2 large staff.
    - #3 work alone if interacting with outside people.
    - #4 work alone, but likes to be around people.
    - #5 work alone but with people interaction.
    - #6 either.
    - #7 work alone.
    - #8 large staff.
    - #9 large staff.

9. **Do you prefer to be organized or with a bit of clutter?**

    - #1 a bit of clutter.
    - #2 organized.
    - #3 a bit of clutter.
    - #4 organized.
    - #5 clutter.
    - #6 organized.
    - #7 organized.
    - #8 organized.
    - #9 a bit of clutter.

10. **Do you prefer a proper color scheme or is color unimportant?.** This item deals with the coordination of the colors, not with the effect of particular colors on the mood.

    - #1 unimportant.
    - #2 proper color scheme vital.
    - #3 color important to mood.
    - #4 unimportant.

- #5 unimportant.
- #6 proper color scheme vital.
- #7 unimportant.
- #8 proper color scheme vital.
- #9 proper color scheme important.

11. **Do you prefer a quiet environment or noise in the background?**

    - #1 some noise from activity.
    - #2 quiet music, general quiet.
    - #3 noise from activity and chatter.
    - #4 some background noise not requiring interaction.
    - #5 lively activity with some noise.
    - #6 quiet hum of conversation.
    - #7 quiet.
    - #8 quiet because everyone is working.
    - #9 some noise with appropriate music.

12. **Do you prefer proper equipment or can you make do?**

    - #1 makes do, and will use whatever is available in novel ways.
    - #2 proper equipment.
    - #3 uses what is available.
    - #4 proper equipment, but can get by with less.
    - #5 uses what is available in novel ways.
    - #6 proper equipment.
    - #7 proper equipment, but can improvise.
    - #8 proper equipment.
    - #9 Makes a scene if lacking, but can get by.

13. **Do you prefer a full plan up front or to plan on the go?**

    - #1 plan on the go, likely to change it.
    - #2 full plan in advance.
    - #3 plan on the go, maybe.
    - #4 plan in advance.
    - #5 What plan?
    - #6 plan in advance.
    - #7 plan on the go.
    - #8 plan in advance.
    - #9 either.

14. **Do you prefer routine or a variety of challenging tasks?**

    - #1 variety of challenging tasks.
    - #2 routine.

- #3 variety of tasks.
- #4 routine.
- #5 never routine.
- #6 either.
- #7 routine as required.
- #8 focused effort.
- #9 variety of tasks.

15. **Do you prefer to figure things out or to consult experts?**

    - #1 figure them out.
    - #2 consult the experts.
    - #3 either.
    - #4 figure them out.
    - #5 either.
    - #6 consult the experts.
    - #7 figure them out.
    - #8 either.
    - #9 figure them out.

16. **Do you work best under pressure or when more relaxed?**

    - #1 under pressure.
    - #2 relaxed.
    - #3 handles either.
    - #4 relaxed.
    - #5 creates own pressure.
    - #6 relaxed.
    - #7 either.
    - #8 pressure.
    - #9 relaxed.

17. **Do you prefer single project at a time or several in the works?**

    - #1 several at once.
    - #2 one at a time.
    - #3 several at once.
    - #4 one at a time.
    - #5 a lot at once.
    - #6 either.
    - #7 one at a time.
    - #8 several in the works by delegating.
    - #9 either.

18. **Do you prefer outside financing or building on own resources?**

- #1 own resources
- #2 financing to hire professionals
- #3 own resources
- #4 own resources
- #5 either depending upon project
- #6 financing to hire professionals
- #7 own resources
- #8 financing to hire professionals
- #9 both

19. **Do you prefer a known field or a new area?**

- #1 new field.
- #2 known well.
- #3 new field.
- #4 known field.
- #5 new field.
- #6 known well.
- #7 new knowledge in known field.
- #8 known field.
- #9 either.

20. **Do you prefer proven area or being a pioneer in a lesser known field?**
- #1 pioneer.
- #2 proven area.
- #3 either.
- #4 proven area.
- #5 pioneer.
- #6 proven area.
- #7 pioneer.
- #8 proven area.
- #9 either.

As you go through the list you will find that most of your preferences can be reasonably accommodated by the numbers of your chart, but the traits that are very set within a number can cause problems. For example: #1 has to take initiative, but #2 is a finisher, not a starter. Or #4 is a routine worker and #5 can't stand routine. You will never get a perfect match on all the core numbers of your business and personal charts. What you are looking for are those glaring inconsistencies.

In some instances opposite extremes can be coordinated with a bridge number. To find the bridge, subtract the smaller from the larger of the discordant numbers. The result will be the bridge needed to coordinate the energies. For example: 2 and 8 are discordant energies. The bridge is a 6. The 2 works behind the scenes with tact and diplomacy, or even by manipulation. The 8 is confrontational and direct. The 6 bridge softens the harshness of the 8 and puts some starch in the backbone of the 2.

Have fun working with the preferences. Play with the combinations until it feels right to you. As you go through the list, begin to visualize your business beginning to take shape.

CHAPTER 13

Expansion

Chapter 3, on the choice of name, briefly mentioned planning for expansion. This chapter goes deeper into the planning possibilities with the numbers. You may be feeling that you are just getting the business started or, with an established business, that you are not ready to expand. You may think this topic is premature, but when you set up the business initially with an expansion potential, you lessen the challenges when you are ready for that step.

Each chapter builds upon the prior chapters like building blocks in a foundation. Some repetition is desirable to remind you of points that otherwise may be overlooked and to present these items from a fuller perspective.

Planning for expansion needs to start at the initial set-up of the business. The first step is to envision how large an organization you wish to build. There is no right or wrong answer as to the scope of your vision. You have already done some thinking about this issue in responding to the Questionnaire. As you have thought about your business, has your desire changed? Did you choose a specific size answer based upon what you felt was a present possibility? Or has your desire enlarged. These are all important considerations.

There are advantages to a small business, perhaps as limited as a sole proprietorship with no employees. There are also advantages to a large corporation that has a global outreach. Your personal numbers go a long way toward determining your ideal choice. You may think that you want the prestige and money that accompanies the CEO of a large corporation when your personal numbers are more suited to a sole proprietorship. You may set up your corporation to be a large player, only to find that you are uncomfortable making the weighty decisions necessary to keep that form of business viable.

On the other hand, you may be destined for major growth, but have set up your business with the energies of a sole proprietorship. You will constantly be stymied by the limitations. Neither of these business types is better than the other. The important consideration is what is right for you. Your personal chart was set at birth. You cannot change it. You can only add nuances to it. By accepting who you are and projecting that person into the business world, you stand a good chance of success. When you struggle to create a business from a different base, you will always seem to be an imposter.

You may want to review Chapter 5 on the legal format. This chapter builds upon that work. The discussion that follows pertains to both your personal chart and the business chart.

Motivation, Talents and Opportunity

Look at the soul urge (total of the vowels) the expression (total of all the letters) and the life path (total of the full birth date or founding date). For the moment, look at the numbers as numbers rather than symbols. Calculate the difference between these numbers by subtracting the smaller from the larger.

Example: a 9 soul urge, a 1 expression and a 4 life path. The difference between the soul urge and the expression is 8. The difference between the soul urge and the life path is 5. The difference between the life path and the expression is 3.

For this process, we count places – 1,2,3,4,5,6,7,8,9,11,22,33,44 (there is one place between each number in this series.)

If you have a master number, count 1 place between 9 and 11, or between 11 and 22. It is 2 places between 11 and 33 and 3 places between 9 and 33. With master numbers you will need to do this procedure for both the master number and the reduced number. You will get different results. Since you do not operate at all times on the master plane, you need to keep in mind the effect when you are working with the reduced energy.

The soul urge number designates the motivation. The expression number designates innate talents and abilities. The life path number designates opportunities.

Starting with the soul urge (9) the motivation is very high. The 1 expression is very low. This person is always reaching beyond himself because of the desire to do more than is comfortable. He must constantly be developing new talents to keep up with the motivation. The motivation is also higher than the opportunities.

As a result, to fulfill the motivation this person must create his own opportunities. This chart has a degree of frustration built into it.

If the opportunities were substantially higher than the motivation, many good chances for success would be lost for lack of interest. If the talents were substantially higher than the motivation this person could lose some of his drive because he would feel that he could coast.

Again, there are no right or wrong numbers. Whatever numbers are in your personal chart serve a purpose in your growth. When you set up your business, you may want to consider closing some of the greater gaps by coming up with compatible numbers to your personal numbers that are closer together. 1 or 2 places is very good. 3 or 4 places is workable. A wider gap may cause challenges. Now understand that challenges aren't necessarily bad as long as you know what you are facing and how to deal with them.

If you are going to be a sole proprietor, you would want a small gap in correlating these 3 numbers because you will be doing it all. The larger an organization you plan the wider the gaps can be because you will be hiring people to fill in what you lack.

Now, going back to the numbers as symbols of energies, the lower numbers tend to be simple energies. The higher value numbers become more complex. The 1, for example is a single number. It has no other components, so is ideal for a sole proprietorship. The 2 can only be derived from 1+1. It is either a straight single number or a master number. It is the number for partnerships. We begin to get complexity with the 3. It can result from 1+2, but it is still a relatively simple energy. By the time we reach the 9, it can result from 1+8, 2+7,

3+6, or 4+5. All of these combinations add up to 9, but each grouping has a different feeling to it. The 1+8 is business and money oriented. The 2+7 is intuitive and sensitive. The 3+6 is artistic and creative. The 4+5 brings a direct conflict into the underlying energy. The ultimate meaning will still be that of the 9 energy, but each with a separate nuance in its application.

The greater complexity of the higher numbers allows the possibility of connections with a more diverse group of employees. These higher numbers are therefore suited to a larger operation.

Some numbers are particularly suited to certain businesses. A larger business has room for more combinations because you would want a wide range of activities.

The small business is more likely to cover a single focus, or a limited number of areas.

Business Types by the Numbers

A brief guide to business activities suited to particular numbers:

- 1- sole proprietorships of all types, but particularly innovative businesses.
- 2- partnerships. arbitrator, negotiator, interior designer, musician (particularly composer), counselor, executive assistant, historian, statesman.
- 3- writer, public speaker, comedian, sales person, politician, minister.
- 4- realtor, accountant, attorney, architect, factory worker, tool and die maker, landscaper, maintenance worker, business planner, organizer, business broker, financial analyst, technical sales, masseur or masseuse.
- 5- multifaceted. Can do about anything. sales person, investigative journalist, party planner, importer, cruise director.
- 6- doctor, nurse, counselor, teacher, alternative medicine practitioner, performer, actor, homemaker, human resources worker, interior decorator, manager.
- 7- scientific researcher, mathematician, philosopher, troubleshooter, technical support person, numerologist, astrologer, astronomer, geneticist, professor, technical writer, statistician.
- 8- manager of a large operation, investor, stock broker.
- 9- philanthropist, head of a not-for-profit organization, community organizer, politician, foundation president, hospital administrator, environmentalist, chaplain.
- 11- (see #2 above) minister, public speaker, statesman, intuitive.
- 22- (see #4 above) business builder on a grand scale.
- 33- (see #6 above) teacher of teachers, master performer.

Obviously, this list is incomplete, but the included occupations give you a sense of the type of businesses that fit each number.

Let's look at an example to show more clearly how the numbers force or limit expansion.

> *You have a business of going grocery shopping for shut-ins or running errands for busy people. You do this on your own for customers that you have generated through flyers, ads and word of mouth. This is a simple sole proprietorship and probably would do well with a strong 1 energy in the chart. Perhaps a 3 would help in the people connections and a 6 to show compassion for the*

needs of those whom you service. You will do some record keeping, vehicle maintenance and route organizing. This is a fairly simple business.

You get enough business that you can no longer handle it all yourself. It is time to hire someone to help out. Now you have added management requirements, route coordination. You see opportunities to add services. You either need to have legal and accounting knowledge or to hire professional services. 4 energy is a help at this stage.

As time goes by, you provide such quality service that you have a staff of several people doing the actual service while you devote yourself to management duties. You hire office staff as well. It becomes desirable to delegate the duties that initially you did yourself. 8 energy becomes important.

You do so well that you decide to franchise the business. Now you need precise systems in place with a full explanation of the practices and procedures. Manuals need to be written. Contracts need to be prepared. Financing becomes necessary. Arbitration procedures for franchisee disputes need to be established. A massive advertising campaign is desirable to support your franchisees. You are approaching the 22 level.

The business has become well established. You decide to do a public offering to sell stock as a means of further financing and expansion. You are into full management mode of the 8 or 22/4.

You set up or purchase additional businesses and place them as a division of your corporation. You now become a conglomerate with a wide range of businesses all working under a single umbrella corporation.

When you are setting up your business, you probably envision some level of growth. If this example were your business, how far down the list would you want to go? A solid plan to get to that level before you start the business will help you to create the right steps at each stage without backtracking and reorganizing.

Chapter 14

Vision

The distinction between the image statement that you did in chapter 11 and the vision statement is a matter of perspective. In simple terms, the image statement is the face that you show the world. The vision statement is the internal view of where your business is heading. The mission statement is a declaration of how your business will treat its employees and customers.

The vision statement and the mission statement are promises. The vision statement is a promise to the business that we will get you to this level. The mission statement is a promise to the public that this is how we will treat you. Both are coordinated to the full business plan, which is a statement of how you intend to reach the goals of the vision statement and to incorporate the promises of the mission statement into the operation of the business.

It may seem at first glance that this chapter has little to do with numerology. Although it does not specifically follow a number list, you have already done the necessary numerology work in prior chapters. The numbers were the base from which you began. If your work in this chapter is not true to the numbers of your personal chart and your business chart, you will not feel a sense of rightness in your statements.

The Vision Statement

The prior chapter incorporated the idea of expansion. How large and/or how complex do you want your business to grow? The vision statement formalizes that level into a promise to reach it. It is your ultimate goal for the business. The vision statement is more than a nice sounding piece of fluff. You are committing to doing everything necessary to reach that level.

The vision statement should be complete enough to show the destination. It is the role of the business plan to show the route you will take to that goal. As an example, it would be an inadequate vision statement to merely state that by a date 5 years hence you want the business to gross a million dollars. You want to include items such as the type of facility you anticipate, the number of employees, the level of expansion and your role in the business.

As you write your vision statement, if you have been honest in your assessment of where you want to go, you will feel a surge of excitement. The possibilities will jump out at you. Be sure to separate the vision from the plan. You may have to revise your work several times to move items into the appropriate document. Your first inclination will probably be to include too much of the plan in the vision.

The vision statement will probably not be a lengthy document 2 or 3 paragraphs is usually adequate. If your statement is much longer than that, you are probably including extraneous items. Make it as tight as you can without eliminating important aspects of your goal. Do the statement in present tense as an accomplished fact rather than as a future prospect. Putting it in as a *fait accompli* will help to engrain it into your thinking and make its accomplishment almost automatic. With the vision statement in place, you will begin to make all your business decisions on the basis of whether or not it is taking you toward your goal.

Example vision statement: Life Path Numerology Center (name the business) is in a 5,000 SF office located in the downtown area close to the business center. It contains 3 separate departments with a department head for each. These departments are personal growth services, business services and education. Each of the departments is self-sustaining and independent of the others, but coordinated in their functions, space and supplies. There is an administrative staff to oversee the operation of the total business. I will continue to teach, create products and make policy. There are satellite offices in 5 other cities that duplicate the Indianapolis operation on the scale necessary for the needs of that area.

The Mission Statement

The mission statement is a promise to your employees, customers and/or clientele about what they can expect from the business. This statement should be based upon the numbers of your personal chart and the business chart. If the numbers of the charts are predominantly service oriented numbers such as 2, 6 and 9, avoid items about providing economical pricing. Stress the caring aspect of the business. If your numbers are business oriented, such as 1, 4 and 8, a caring statement will ring false.

The mission statement will probably be shorter than the vision statement. Try to fit it into a single paragraph. Some businesses have a very effective mission statement in a single sentence. The mission statement needs to remain consistent. It must reflect how you actually run the business. Too often you have seen mission statements that were at odds with your experience of the business. You know...a communication company that puts you through menu hoops without a means to actually talk with a live person, but invites you to call for service. You likely dismiss the statement as a meaningless bit of propaganda. When that situation occurs, you likely also lose a degree of respect for that business.

I have found it best to use specific, active words. Take a look at Google's mission statement:

Google's mission is to organize the world's information and make it universally accessible and useful.

It is short and to the point, yet says all that really needs to be said.

As with many larger corporations, Google goes on to add additional sections on integrity, core values, etc. but the statement itself is quite succinct. Adding a lot of platitudes that have no real meaning, waters down the statement. Hype in a mission statement does not move you any more than you would be persuaded by hype in ad copy. My rule of thumb is if it needs proof it should not be part of the mission statement. This document is not a promotional piece. It is a statement of what to expect when dealing with the business.

For a company in its mission statement to say that we are the best or the greatest, or we will treat you right, is meaningless. What does it mean to this business to be the best – that is what should be included. What does it specifically mean to treat you right. Spell it out.

The Google statement, if fulfilled, will make them the best and their customers will be treated right. It includes the specific reasons that anyone would use a search engine. How well has Google fulfilled their mission statement? The volume of hits would say that consumers of their service consistently think they do a good job.

That is the type of mission statement that you want. It provides a statement of intent. The evaluation is up to the employees and the public.

Benjamin Franklin in writing to a widow friend said that if he had more time, he would have written a shorter letter. It is easy to ramble on. To say precisely what you mean in few words takes a great deal of care. Rewrite your statement until it sends the appropriate message without fluff. This chapter may seem to be brief, but to craft the best statements is going to take time and effort. Any effort that you make to get just the right statements will pay dividends in your business.

The Business Plan

The business plan contains the steps necessary to get to the vision. For internal purposes, your plan is a blueprint. It is not a business plan for financing. A business plan for financing has specific detailed requirements that may not be necessary for internal use. You can find outlines and discussions on the sections for a financing business plan by doing a search.

You can do the more thorough plan if you think you will need it. Our purpose here is to create a step-by-step plan to reach your vision.

If you want a 10 story office building to house your expanded business, you probably would not put that as step 1. Understand how you want to grow your business and the order of that growth. It is okay to set time goals for the completion of certain milestones as a means of keeping on track, but don't skip steps just to stay on schedule. Expand the timeline if needed.

As you go along, it will be desirable to modify your plan. You may hire a coach who moves you faster than you had anticipated or you may have setbacks that delay your progress. The plan is more flexible than the vision or mission statements. You should only modify those statements with careful consideration of changing circumstances or to correct inadequacies. When you reach your vision an expansion of the vision statement may be appropriate. Be very careful about reducing your vision because the going is rougher than anticipated. Your job is to find a way to reach the vision. You don't need to do it all yourself. Obtaining help is not cheating. This assistance could be from freelancers, coaches, service companies or employees and any other available resource.

To set up the business plan, list all the items necessary for the conduct of the business at the level of each step. For example, initially you will be doing most of the work yourself. If you are including the financial record keeping in step 1, you may show the function with you providing this service. By the time you get to step 3 or 4, you may have that function listed as an outsourced item or with a secretary to take care of the books. By step 5 you may hire an accountant or business service.

It seems to me that the object of the plan is to move as quickly as is feasible to delegating the routine tasks. You are then free to run the business and raise it to the next level.

Each business is different. Each person starting a business is different. Your plan does not need to look like any other plan. Keep your objective in mind, and the steps will follow in a logical order. Prepare the steps according to how you work best. Your personal integrative vision number will be the primary key to the style. Consider the integrative vision number of the business to determine if it is harmonious or discordant with your personal integrative vision number. If they are different, the tendency is to follow the personal number by default.

There is a lot of work to do in this chapter. It is easy to give this part a lick and a promise and move on to something else. You skip the work of this chapter at your peril. You are building a foundation. A weak base will not support the grand superstructure that you envision. Good luck in creating just the right documents for your business.

CHAPTER 15

Style

This chapter covers the physical face of your business. It includes the effect of the business address, the telephone numbers, the physical appearance of your work place and the décor. It also includes the color scheme for your office, logo, stationery and vehicles.

As you work through these details by the numbers, you should begin to feel a sense of rightness. You will have a solid picture of what you are putting together. If any part of the image is not comfortable to you, determine if there is a conflict in the numbers with which you are dealing. You may need to tweak that item by adding a nuance from other numbers in the chart or by creating a bridge number to coordinate the conflict. As you will recall from a previous lesson, to get a bridge number between two conflicting numbers, subtract the smaller number from the larger. The difference is the bridge. Bring in some of the qualities of the bridge. Does that addition now make the element feel more comfortable?

Business Address

The Street Number

The delineation principle that applies to physical numbers in your business is that the numbers that are the least shared are the strongest. So for the address, consider the digits first. Fewer entities share that number. If you are in a building or complex that has an umbrella address for several suites, the suite number or letter is an add-on to the address. According to the principle, we might think that the suite number is the strongest energy. However, the suite number does not stand alone. It is a modifier to the base address.

First add the street number digits and get a total. The assumption with a suite number present is that this address is shared by several offices. If the suite is designated by a letter, convert the suite letter to its number value. Do not add the words "suite" or "Apartment" or other designation into the calculation.

Evaluate the base energy of the address for a fit to your business. The suite number adds nuances to that base number. It tells you how to develop the energy of the base address. Coordinate the digits total not including the suite number with your charts.

Marketers will sometimes use a suite number to designate a specific campaign. Different suite numbers may be used for the same ad in different publications. When a response comes in under that suite number, it shows the source of the response. When a suite number is used in this manner, I tend to ignore it as not a true part of the address. It could be a good research project to determine whether certain suite numbers pull better.

Example: 1506 North Meridian Street, Suite A. The digits total 1+5+0+6=12=3. The "A" of the suite converts to a 1. The 3 address can be a bit scattered and irresponsible with money. The 1 energy of the suite number brings a discipline to the 3 without killing the excitement of social contacts.

The Street Name and Beyond

The energy of the street name is more diffuse than the digits because more entities share this energy. The question in working with an appropriate energy is how far you go. The street name should probably be considered. Convert the name to number values. If you need the reference, the conversion table is on the calculation sheet. The resulting street name number should also be harmonious with the chart energies. In delineating the street name, do not include designations such as north, south, east or west, street, avenue, boulevard, etc. unless it is a distinctive part of the street name, such as in Rodeo Drive or Sunset Boulevard.

When choosing a location for the business, the city and state should be considered, but not as the primary determinant. Indianapolis is a 6 city; Indiana is a 7 state. There is a built in conflict between the state and the city that is noticeable. Indianapolis is the capitol, but much of the rest of the state seems to be in opposition. This conflict will not affect your business as personally as the closer terms of the address. If you find the city of your choice brings too much conflict to your chart numbers, you may consider a suburb with a more compatible number.

The postal code containing a large number of entities is diffuse. If you are looking for a perfect match, you might try for a zip code that is harmonious with your chart numbers. When doing this analysis, you need to determine how fine-tuned you want to be. My rule of thumb is if you are choosing a state for relocation, choose a compatible number. To determine the city or suburb look at the numbers. If you are already in that location, the difference may not be significant enough to relocate. Look most strongly to the street address.

Example: 1506 North Meridian Street. Indianapolis, Indiana 46204. Digits = 3; Meridian = (46) (10) 1; Indianapolis = 6; Indiana = 7; 46204 = 16/7.

Telephone Numbers

The primary telephone considerations are the numbers specific to your business. In the USA the first three numbers are the area code, which covers a wide area and a lot of telephones, so it is of lesser concern. The second set of three numbers covers an exchange, which is less diffuse. The last four digits are specifically assigned. They are the numbers that will be most significant. You can pick up nuances by combining the exchange and the specific number for an added overlay.

Example: 317-638-9752. 9752 = 23 = 5; 638 = 17 = 8; 5+8=13/4. The 5 tends to be chatty, so adding the 4 total tempers the wild conversation of the 5 energy.

Effect of the Telephone Numbers

The reduced number of the last four digits will determine the nature of the calls. You want compatibility to your charts. If you are a friendly, outgoing person and your business reflects this style, you probably would not be comfortable with a 4 telephone number, which indicates short, to the point calls.

If your number reduces to:

1- Calls will include new ideas. You will likely dominate the call.
2- Calls will be filled with emotion and consideration, often with difficulty getting to the point.
3- Calls will contain a lot of social content. It may be difficult to conclude the call.
4- Calls will be all business with little chit-chat.
5- Calls will be upbeat and often off on a tangent.
6- Calls will be balanced between business and social content; a good mix.
7- Calls will be inconsistent. At times the social content will dominate and at others, there can be an abrupt conclusion.
8- Calls will be strongly business, but without the terseness of the 4. They will cover a broader view.
9- Calls will often be emotional and idealistic.
11- Calls will be of an encouraging and enlightening nature, often with spiritual content.
22- Calls will be at a high level of business. Much of the content will be on how to expand the business.
33- Calls will have a teaching component. They could often be lengthy.

Work Space Environment

In the chapter on Image and Preferences you developed the feel of the office or shop. You have a picture of whether it should be elegant or casual; rigid or flexible; hierarchical or family like; large or small; at home or away; etc.

Now let's add a color scheme and an operational style. Each number has its own emphasis. To come up with the appropriate balance, take your main elements from the life path and the expression. Bring in elements of the soul urge number as a secondary emphasis and add touches from the personality and birthday numbers.

The Styles for the Numbers

- #1– ideas are more important than the environment. Probably non-traditional furnishings. Flexible hours and management style, but top down control.
    - Color suggestions: red tones
- #2– all must be in harmony and good taste. Warm environment, likely to include antiques. Cooperative management style. Confrontation discouraged. May encourage personal emotional involvement. Don't let manipulative actions get out of hand. Rule by committee.
    - Color suggestions: orange tones, earth colors and heavy wood

- #3– Light and airy. Conversation encouraged. Modern furnishings. Open door policy. Input from employees welcome.
    - Color suggestions: Yellow tones
- #4– Traditional, but efficient work space. Few frills. Furnishings functional, rather than elegant. Organization and systems emphasized. Routine favored. Set ways of doing things. Business controlled by written policy.
    - Color suggestions: Green tones
- #5– Modern décor. Easily moved furnishings, often rearranged for the needs of the moment. Light and airy. Freedom is a value. Business needs to operate beyond the limits of the office – take the show on the road.
    - Color suggestions: Blue tones
- #6– Comfortable, homey atmosphere, with all in good taste. Nothing gaudy. Eclectic mix of modern and antiques. Each included piece likely has a special meaning to someone in the office.
    - Color suggestions: Indigo
- #7– An atmosphere conducive to research. In depth discussions on specific topics. Traditional furnishings. Quiet noise level. Serious study.
    - Color suggestions: Purple, mauve, violet
- #8– An elegant showplace. Only the finest quality should be included. The business has a strong hierarchical structure with a dominant leader. Laziness or sloppy work is not tolerated. Money and finances are a major force.
    - Color suggestions: Rose
- #9– All in good taste. Seeking the ideal. Warm atmosphere. Strong, but understanding, leader. Traditional furnishings in classic styles.
    - Color suggestions: yellow-gold

Reduce the master numbers for this purpose.

Example: 3 life path; 6 expression; 8 soul urge; 2 personality, 4 birthday. The 3 life path requires a light and airy feeling. The 6 expression demands good taste, and can be eclectic. I would strive for a traditional style, not antiques, upholstered in the colors of the 3. The 8 soul urge adds the need for quality, and can fit the chosen style. Accent the décor with a single or very few antique vases or other period pieces to bring in the 2 personality. Finish it off by incorporating a proper work flow into the design to fit the 4 of the birthday.

The colors used in the décor will strengthen the aspects of the number to which it associates. If you want a stronger emphasis upon the accomplishment of the purpose, strengthen the color of the life path. If the motivation needs shoring up, add more of the color of the soul urge.

Try to use the colors of all the core numbers in the degree of the core number strengths.

Example using the same core as above: 3 Life Path – yellow, 6 expression – indigo, 8 soul urge – Rose, 2 personality – orange, and 4 birthday - green.

In this example, I would paint the walls a pale yellow, with furniture upholstered in indigo fabric or leather. Add a large Rose tree in a corner (artificial could work, but better if live). Perhaps a rosewood end table with green plants and finished off with orange and green throw pillows. Add a dark green carpet. Use your own imagination. The important elements are the colors and the amount of each color for appropriate balance with the chart. If there is discord in the numbers, you may get mismatches in the colors. Try to blend them by careful choice of tones and amount used.

Choose a single color for the company identification. With 1 energy. Life path Numerology Center has chosen burgundy (a shade of red) for the logo, stationery, and décor.

CHAPTER 16

Hiring

When you get to the point of hiring additional help, this chapter could be worth the entire cost of the book Having the right people working with you is a key element of a successful business. You don't want to bring in someone who will be disruptive to the business or who will quickly burn out. It is expensive to hire and train employees. If they leave or you need to fire them in short order, you have wasted the time, effort and money invested in them.

With numerology you can know in advance that your new hiree will likely work out in the long term. Working with a military recruiter, we did an extensive comparison between numerology and the Myers-Briggs test. The results were consistently in agreement. When it is a major position that you are filling, you may want to use several testing methods, including the standard psychological tests, the Myers-Briggs, the Minnesota preference test, etc. But you may find that numerology can give you a fuller picture of the person without the added delay for the test results.

You probably would not need as full a report on a person that you hire for specific projects on an *ad hoc* basis. It would be unlikely that you would require a battery of tests on someone whom you hire to create a web site or to produce ad copy, but wouldn't it be desirable to have some idea of the person's work habits, attention to detail and cooperation? Numerology can give you that information quickly.

Preliminary Considerations

In Chapter 13 you looked at your goals for expansion. Keep this level in mind before you hire your first employee. This prior work will give perspective in filling the position. How will this person fit into the total picture that you are trying to create?

Don't be too quick to add staff. Put it off as long as is feasible. Hiring an employee is a major step. You move out of the simple structure of a sole practitioner. With one employee, you become involved with a new level of benefits and taxes. Your relationship with government entities becomes more complex. Your legal obligations are increased. In addition, you are making a major commitment to another person. It is not a situation that you can try and easily discontinue if it doesn't work out.

When you need to add a position to your business or seek to fill an existing position, first consider how thoroughly you need to investigate the candidates. The following list includes some of the items to evaluate:

How much training is required to do the job? A position that does not require much training needs a less thorough evaluation than a policy making position. For most jobs above routine work, the average time to really learn the job is about six months. For those jobs, you don't want to invest three or four months of development, only to have the person become discouraged and leave.

How much responsibility does the position include? You want to be confident of your decision in hiring a candidate who will be a part of your business' public face. For people on the front line, you should dig a little deeper.

Is this position a step into higher management levels? These people need to be more strongly vetted.

Consider your business position as well. A start up business just beginning expansion should be more careful. A single employee may be asked to handle a wide variety of functions. If the candidate is not versatile enough, there may be gaps in the coverage.

Specific Candidate Considerations

When you put out a call to fill a position, you can expect a large response, particularly when unemployment rates are high. Get through the preliminary screening quickly. If you have resumes or written applications, you can immediately eliminate several applicants just from the written presentation. Meeting the candidates face to face will eliminate a number more. You may feel that their appearance is not a match. I am not talking about race or gender issues. They may not dress appropriately for the position. For a higher level job you expect a business dress standard. For a warehouse position, you may be leery of someone who arrives dressed in a suit and tie.

A live meeting also allows you to do an intuitive evaluation. In chapter 9, you worked with the quick check based only upon the first name or name used in the introduction. The Quick Check should not by itself rule someone out, but it does give clues as to whether you want to pursue this candidate further.

The Personal Year Cycle

The calculation instructions for finding the personal year are in chapter 2 (add together the digits of the month and day of birth or the founding date for the business. Reduce the total and add that number to the digits of the current year). When you have whittled down the list, be sure that you have the birth date of the remaining prospects. The starting point will be the personal year cycle. If the prospect's cycle is incompatible with the cycle of the business, be careful in hiring that person. The incompatibility will cause burnout. For some it may take a while to become evident. Others will feel it almost immediately. No matter how perfect this candidate looks for your business or the position, that person will not fulfill his or her potential. This person will always be at odds with the flow of your business.

The personal year cycle may not seem to be that important up front. I have known people who have worked in incompatible businesses for several years with apparent good results. They could function adequately with the conflict, but when they were finally released to seek out a more conducive position, they blossomed like they could not under the restraints of the numbers. Although adequate, they were producing at a level well under their potential. This circumstance was not optimal for either the individual or the business.

Full Chart Comparisons

Once you have narrowed the field to the best of the crop, it is time to do an in-depth review. To run a full chart requires the full name at birth. You may be reticent to ask for this information. Some of your prospects may bolt at that point. You must determine how far you want to go.

Because we are a numerology center, it is easy for us to explain and justify this request. Because I believe in the benefits of numerology in business and have seen the results in client businesses, my attitude would be to ask for the data without hesitation. If the prospect is really interested in the job, he or she may think it weird to give this information, but most of them will accommodate the process.

A lot of your success in getting the data depends upon your attitude in requesting it. If you treat it as a routine part of the process, the prospect won't question it either. If you approach it hesitantly you will get questions as to why you need this data. I have found the easiest way to make the request is to include a line on the application form for the full name at birth. The printed form implies that this is a routine question.

I like to be up front with prospects by telling them that we evaluate hirees by using numerology. In our case we use numerology in lieu of psychological tests, Myers-Briggs tests and preference tests. Numerology gives us the information to make an informed decision without the delay and expense of other testing.

Run the full chart on your remaining prospects. You will begin to see patterns of the numbers. I recommend placing the data in chart form using the name of each prospect as a column head. Title the rows according to the core numbers in descending order of strength as in the following sample. Create as many columns as you need for the number of prospects.

Use the Aspect Table and the Meaning of Numbers from the Appendix to make the comparisons.

Core #	Business	Name 1	Name 2	Name 3	Name 4	Name 5
Integrative Vision						
Life Path						
Expression						
Soul Urge						
Personality						
Birth day						

By also including the numbers from your business chart you have a clear visual image of the comparison. You could also add another column for your own personal numbers if you wish.

If you find a lot of conflicting numbers in the chart of a prospect, that person may not be your first choice. But you do need to consider the needs of the position. Your business numbers may not have a lot of nuts and bolts business energy, but for a bookkeeper, you may want someone whose energies supports working with detail.

In some positions you may want to hire someone who fills a needed function that is not a strong part of the business chart. You still want a basic compatibility, but perhaps with a nuance of missing energies.

CHAPTER 17

Personnel

In the prior chapter we discussed the hiring of new personnel. In this lesson we look at the staff that are already or will be a part of your business.

Numerology is not an automatic template. It gives you the base for making better decisions. In the course of your business operation, situations may arise where you are forced to go against the numbers, such as in the timing of events. If the numbers say that it is not the most appropriate time to perform a particular task, but you have a deadline to meet, you may need to push through the project anyway. If it is not a good social day, but necessity demands that you attend an important meeting, you go. But to the extent that it is possible, following the numbers will produce the best results.

As your business expands, you need to think about the various functions that you and your staff will need to perform. Initially all the roles will fall upon your shoulders. You will do some of them well and eagerly. Other tasks will not be comfortable for you.

Number Characteristics that Apply to the Functions

For more detail see the number meanings page.

1- Independent thinker, not a conformist, takes action on own initiative, (group leader, independent contractor)
2- Takes care of details, follows behind others and completes what is unfinished, a sympathetic ear, non-confrontational, (executive secretary, negotiator, decorator)
3- Communicator, sales ability, teacher, trainer. (sales staff or management, sales trainer, public relations)
4- Detail oriented, organized, rigid. (real estate and legal matters, bookkeeping, routine production)
5- A maverick, easily bored, free spirit, needs constant activity, impulsive. (outside sales person, advertising, importer)
6- Multifaceted, creative, responsible, nurturing, calming influence. (teacher, sales)
7- Analytical, problem solver, deep thinker, nonconformist. (techie, lab worker, researcher)

8- High level management, demanding, trustworthy, money management. (BOSS, leader, financier)
9- Altruistic, Perfectionist, idealist, leader. (head of philanthropic organization, leader of causes, artist, advertiser)
11- see also the 2 entry. Visionary, ethical, brings spiritual perspective to business. (motivational speaker)
22- see also the 4 entry. Master builder, planner, major projects, large vision. (project head, planning coordinator)
33- see also the 6 entry. Master teacher, performer, healing arts, care giver. (teacher, almost any position)

Remember that the chart will contain a combination of numbers, some of which may be in conflict. Give appropriate strength to the core numbers. The order of strength is integrative vision, life path, expression, soul urge, personality and birth day. Read the stronger first modified by the weaker.

I would recommend starting with these **broad categories**:

Business Functions

- Legal aspects and accounting
- Policy making
- Management
- Bookkeeping and secretarial duties
- Marketing, sales and sales management
- Production, If the business creates its own products, distribution and delivery of products and services
- Customer service, may include "tech" support

Determine which functions excite you. These areas probably use your best skills. Unfamiliar areas that use your weaker skills are the functions that you should first farm out. No badges are given for forcing yourself to learn jobs that you dislike doing. You are not in danger of becoming a failure if you choose not to do everything yourself. It is important to have a general grasp of all the functions in order to direct the jobs that you delegate.

Legal and Accounting

Unless you have a legal or accounting background, it is probably advisable to seek counsel in these areas initially. You want your business to be on a sound footing from the start. An attorney will prepare the appropriate legal papers and advise you on specific requirements of the state and federal laws. You don't want to invest a lot of time, effort and money into building the business only to have it crash because of an overlooked vital provision. An accountant can set up your books so that your record keeping meets the necessary standards for tax purposes. Many times competent counsel can save you more money than the cost.

When working with attorneys and accountants, you will save on the fees by doing as much of the work as you can. Use these professionals to do the initial set-ups and consultation as needed.

Choosing an Attorney - You are not seeking a trial attorney. Should court action at some later time become necessary, your regular business attorney will use co-counsel. The skills needed in a good business attorney differ from those needed for trial work. In working with professionals you will have difficulty obtaining any information to develop a chart. Use the quick check (see Chapter 9.) If you can get the birth date, you can at least determine that he or she is on a compatible cycle.

My recommendation is to work with a fairly young attorney. He likely will be around for a long time and can grow with your business. His rates will be lower and you will probably be less intimidated than you would be by a well-known business attorney in a major firm. By explaining to your choice that you want to work with him for a long time, you can lead in to asking for the birth date. If you are comfortable disclosing that you want the information for numerology use, you will learn a lot about how he reacts to other areas as well.

Choosing an Accountant – The same considerations apply to an accountant as to an attorney. You do not want to use a highly paid accountant to do the regular bookkeeping. You should do that work in house and submit the results to your accountant on a quarterly or annual basis, depending upon whether a quarterly estimated return is necessary.

Consider your risk taking comfort level. Although accounting may seem to be a cut and dried profession, there is a lot of leeway between accountants who want to take any conceivable tax deduction and those who stay well within the guidelines to avoid any possible challenge. Too cutting edge an accountant can land you in hot water, requiring time and cost to meet the challenges. Too cautious an accountant can cost you a higher tax bill than is necessary. Find a match for your style.

Strong 4 energy will usually designate a conservative attorney or accountant. 6 energy is well-balanced. A person with 6 energy is more likely to be middle of the road. 5 and 3 energy designate a risk taker who may be slipshod in his approach. 1 energy would designate a professional who has innovative ideas that work. With 8 energy your work will likely be delegated to staff, which is usually okay as long as you are not charged the top professional rate.

Business Functions

Policy Making – It is up to you to set the policies for your business. In an earlier lesson you developed your preferences and coordinated them to the numbers. Now is the time to write out a consistent statement to guide you and your staff as a foundation for the operation of your business. It is okay to consider input from others, but only accept what matches your desires for the business.

Management – Initially your business will have a boss and a staff, all consisting of a total of one – you! Start the business with solid principles in place for smooth growth. Manage yourself as if you were staff. If management is not your forte, i.e. you are too lax in follow through, before your business grows enough to hire another position, consider a coach to keep you on track. The right coach can make a world of difference; the wrong person in this position can be a disaster. As with anyone with whom you work closely, get as much data as you can to run a chart. For this service, being on the same or a compatible cycle is vital. If your coach is in an incompatible cycle he or she will not be in sync with you or your business. The timing of the recommendations may be inappropriate for you.

Operational Functions

Bookkeeping and Secretarial – These functions require someone who is detail oriented. Many of the tasks included in these functions can be handled by lower skilled employees. It is tempting to hire a student part-time to do the filing, appointment records and financial entries. These jobs probably are not your best use of time. Just remember that even bringing in a lower level part-timer requires all the legal ramifications of having an employee.

Marketing, Sales and Sales Management - No business can thrive without some means of reaching the market and persuading that market to spend money with it. A service oriented business can get by more easily with word of mouth promotion. If you are selling a tangible product, marketing and sales are vital functions. Although 5 and 3 energy are excellent for sales people, you will need to keep tight rein on the finances. The 3 is often illogical in spending and the 5 sees spending more as the primary means of quick sales.

Advertising is such a vital function that we will have a full chapter on the topic later. The numbers allow a sales manager to quickly see what motivates each sales person by determining the soul urge. Although it may seem unlikely, not everyone is motivated by money. In many organizations the sales contests are actually a disincentive to greater production. The top dogs will usually win the big prizes and the rest don't even try. By providing tailored bonuses for certain production levels you are more likely to get the best out of each individual. There is no requirement that the same offer must be made to everyone. Not only can individual bonuses be created, there is no requirement that the value of the rewards be equal, but they should be related to the effort required for the individual to meet the goal.

A marketing or sales person should probably be one of the early additions to your staff. If you have a good product that is well received by the market you may be able to hire a commissioned sales person without busting the budget. Other alternatives are to use outside marketing sources. For an on-line business model, a well-crafted affiliate program could fill the bill.

Production and Distribution of Products – Production includes the entire gamut of obtaining the products for sale. It could mean purchasing at wholesale for resale. It may be digital products that you write or have written for you. It could be an affiliate product. It could be a factory where you are producing a tangible product. Each of these business models requires the appropriate personnel. The prior discussions give you the procedure for the appropriate persons for each of the necessary positions, including management.

Public Relations - for this function, you want someone who has good communication skills, but who is not a maverick. The 6 energy is an ideal match. If your business requires technical support, you may need to split this function. 1 and 7 energy would give the analysis and creative skills to work through the problems.

Promoting Staff

As your business grows, you may be faced with a decision between two or more qualified employees for an upgrade position. Often this type of decision is made based upon personal connections. "I am going to promote John because he is my golf partner." or any other such reason. This may create a congenial working relationship, but it may not be the best choice for business success. By running the numbers and getting the best match for the position and the nature of the responsibilities, you increase the success potential. Using numerology charts also gives you an objective way to show the candidates why a particular choice was made. It removes the taint of cronyism from the decision.

Caution

The primary caution is that you refrain from expanding into additional staff until it becomes necessary. There can be an ego boost to owning a larger operation with a variety of staff people, but an ego based business is not going to be around for long. Your job is to maximize the profits and cash flow and to minimize the costs within the bounds of providing quality products and/or services.

Chapter 18

Vendors

Using the numbers to select a vendor that is right for you is beneficial, but not always easy. Obtaining the necessary data presents a challenge. How much research you do depends upon how important the role of that vendor is to your business and how you do business with that vendor.

Your relationship with a vendor is for the specific purpose of obtaining product or supplies. Because you are not as involved as with an employee or business partner, the analysis need not be as thorough. Key vendors deserve a close review.

Most businesses choose vendors on the basis of how well they like a particular salesperson or that the contact was made just when the need arose. Vendors chosen in this manner may be adequate, but once you are in the habit of using a vendor, deficiencies are often overlooked. It is easier to live with less than optimum service or product than to make a change. You may continue with a vendor from habit.

Dealing with vendors requires a different viewpoint from other interactions. Your primary goal is to obtain the best products at a fair price with little hassle.

Considerations in Categorizing Vendors:

1. Is this a one-time purchase or will you use this vendor repeatedly.
2. What is the cost of the supplied product.
3. How vital is the purchase to your business.
4. Is the product for long term use or is it a throwaway item.
5. How urgent is the delivery time.
6. Are you dealing with a "rep" or directly with the company by mail or online.
7. Are you ordering for future delivery or picking up the purchase from a store.

Obviously, you need to do a deeper analysis of the vendor for important purchases. When you are going into a place of business to make an immediate purchase, it probably doesn't much matter if your relationship ends when you leave the site.

For vendors with whom you will do business on a continuing basis, particularly for materials that are vital to the operation of your business, you need a better method of choice than trial and error.

The numbers do not replace your due diligence; they are a part of it. Even if the numbers are favorable, but the company has a history of poor service or products, avoid them. A company that consistently goes against their own numbers will not be around long.

- For primary suppliers you want a vendor who is reliable. With these suppliers you need to consider both the numbers of the company and of the representative with whom you are dealing. If the company pans out, but the representative is less than desirable, it is appropriate to ask to be serviced by someone else. You will no doubt be asked for a reason, but if they want your business, no reason need be given.
- if you are ordering on line or from a catalogue, you want at least a quick check of the name. It would be difficult to find more data.

What to Look For in Vendors' Numbers

Most vendor charts will have several numbers, some may be in conflict. Remember the order of the strength of the numbers and give first consideration to the strongest numbers. The weaker numbers can point out potential problem areas

>Integrative Vision Number – How the vendor approaches business.
>Life Path Number – The business purpose.
>Expression – What traits predominate?
>Soul Urge – What motivates this vendor?
>Personality – The first impression.
>Birth Day – an obvious trait.

It is not so important to match the vendor numbers with your chart. You are looking for a supplier. If the vendors' numbers match your numbers, the rapport may be better, but the match would not affect the quality of the product or service. You can do business with companies that seem to be less than optimal, but the numbers will tell you where to be wary.

1- Works independently and creatively. You can probably find a way to cut a deal that might not be possible with other numbers.
2- This vendor is not confrontational. Expect negotiation. Watch out for manipulation.
3- Expect a lot of extraneous chatter. A glib use of words may prevent you from asking for necessary details. Very persuasive.
4- Be prepared for a full lay out of facts and figures. Details are important to these vendors. Honesty is a strong point.
5- Be sure you have enough facts. This vendor could take risks and cut corners. A written agreement may be needed for your protection.
6- A good solid balance between friendliness and business talk. Reliable. Expect quality.
7- Misunderstandings can arise after the fact, not through deliberate misleading, but because too much was assumed. Communication can be a problem.

8- Expect the transaction to be solid and businesslike. You will probably pay full price. Expect full value from this vendor.
9- This vendor may be hard to pin down. The perfectionism of the 9 means that the transaction is well defined. The generous nature may allow you to negotiate a better deal.
11- See #2 The 11 may not be entirely practical. This vendor works intuitively and may not always have a stated reason for a decision.
22- See #4 This vendor understands your grand plans and is willing to work with you to fulfill them.
33- See #6 Expect detailed instructions on the use of the product or service.

CHAPTER 19

Distributors

Working with distributors is a part of your marketing. Initially you may do all the promotion yourself or just use an on-line method. When you are ready, using additional distribution channels can multiply your effectiveness.

Not all products and services lend themselves well to some of the listed resources. Consider this lesson a starting point, not a complete guide.

Your relationship with distributors is often more direct than with suppliers. Your customers likely will not be aware of your supply sources. Distributors are a front line for your products and services to your customers. You want to be sure that they have integrity.

Categories of Distributors:

1. Joint venture partners
2. Affiliates
3. Retail outlets
4. Distribution houses
5. Clickbank
6. EBay and Craig's list

In addition to a number match, your choices will be based upon the nature of your product or service, your budget and your comfort zone.

As with all aspects of your business, how detailed you go with the numbers will depend upon the importance of the distributor to your business. Priority, of course, would be given to those who will become long term distributors. The least consideration would be given to one time projects.

A Joint Venture Partner is a company or individual who has an established market that matches your best customers. The promotions are usually at an agreed percentage of the sales or a cross promotion of a single product. Joint venture partners differ from an affiliate in that the joint venture partner is not involved in an ongoing promotion of your products. It may be through an ad in a newsletter or a solo mailing. The agreement with a joint venture partner can be modified for each promotion and is not at a standard affiliate rate. The percentage is negotiable depending upon the benefit you expect to get from the promotion. In some instances you may agree to a 100% payout in order to capture the names and e-mail addresses of the purchasers for your own future promotions. Joint venture partners with whom you wish repeated promotions should have as thorough a review as possible from the available data. If it is critical, you may want to ask directly for the information to run a full chart.

Cross promotions are often dependent upon both sides having reasonably equal databases. Don't expect a major marketer to do a cross promotion if you cannot offer a product or service that is a good match to his customers and that he has a reasonable expectation of obtaining an expansion of his base from your customers. Most major marketers are very selective in joint ventures, so this approach will not be your first line of distribution. Joint ventures can work well even at start-up if you limit your approach to businesses that are at your level.

Affiliates are companies or individuals who have entered into an affiliate contract with you. They promote your products or services for a fixed percentage of the sale price. You will be expected to provide promotional material and credit card processing capability. Affiliates may promote the full range of your products that are included in the affiliate program. They are not bound by a specific timing of the promotions as with a joint venture partner. You can get a good sense of which affiliates will promote your products consistently by having compatible numbers.

Retail Outlets would be available for tangible products. You could be a supplier to the store, or you may need to place the product on consignment. Usually the percentage discount is greater for items that the store purchases up front and less for a consignment order. For a retail store, you probably will not need to do much with the numbers. You get a good view of their operation when you visit. For remote locations, if you want to get paid, you may need more data.

Printed products can be sold through **Distribution Houses** such as New Leaf or any of the on-line bookstores. The two most used are Amazon and Barnes & Nobles. With any of these centers you can expect to give about a 55% discount. They resell to bookstores that get 40%. Added to the discount, you pay the shipping and packaging. Don't expect to get rich through this channel. It is a valid means of getting your product known. There are only a few such distributors, so if you use the better known houses, you probably don't need to run the numbers.

Clickbank is similar to an affiliate program. Once you have submitted your product, you have little control over who picks it up. When an order is placed, Clickbank buys the product from you at a discount and resells it to the purchaser and pays affiliate commission, if appropriate.

There are other similar programs on the internet. Most are reputable, but some are questionable. With the lesser known companies, run the numbers.

Craig's List and eBay are in a category by themselves. If you like working in this environment, you don't have much choice. Both are known to be reliable, so the numbers will probably not be your deciding factor.

For distributors, the compatibility of the numbers with your own business chart is more important than with suppliers, but not as vital as for employees and associates. There are certain number considerations of which to be aware.

A distributor with a strong:

1. Works independently and creatively. You won't need to do a lot of hand-holding.
2. Not confident in proceeding without detailed instructions and encouragement. Avoids confrontation. Best in written promotions or internet.
3. May be slipshod in the paper work, but great at selling. Best in face to face selling.
4. All the details will be in order, a self-starter does not need your push. Solid facts and figures selling. Best at technical products.
5. Similar to the 3. Will probably reach a widespread market. Be wary of a strong 14/5. if working negatively, could be irresponsible or even dishonest.
6. Particularly effective in medical, teaching and home products or self-development services. Best in low key face to face contacts.
7. Needs detailed instructions, and even then may have miscommunication. An effective distributor once the process is down pat. Can be witty and charming, but best using technology.
8. Money motivated. Needs a good deal to go for it. Good sales manager.
9. A great distributor for products or services that have a strong social or green component. A good distributor for performance tickets and fundraising. Likes personal contact.

Chapter 20

Sales

The sales approach has two main components: 1. the content of your sales message and 2. the method of approach to each customer or client. Proper sales and marketing are vital to your business success, but even using the numbers for the best result will require a degree of trial and error. It is said that half of your advertising dollar is wasted; the problem is that no one knows which half! No matter what advertising you do, testing is important. Without adequate tracking of the results you will not know for sure which ad or which style is bringing in the business. If you don't track you could easily make a wrong assumption about the effectiveness of any method.

Advertising can be approached from a scientific base, or it can be a constant experiment. Intuitive people may feel that their gut will guide them appropriately. They may be right. Adding the numbers to developed business methods can be a test of your intuition. Using numerology or any of the other metaphysical sciences tends to enhance and develop your intuition. Since both the numbers and your intuition stem from the energy of the universe, the two work together. Your intuition follows the numbers. When you get a numerology reading, you will reject it if the message does not agree with your intuition and experience.

There is nothing magical about the numbers in advertising. Using the numbers requires a solid analysis. You will still do a certain amount of trial and error. If you follow the numbers and you are not getting results, you may be trying to reach the wrong market with the wrong product or service. An example would be trying to promote gardening tools and supplies to a list of apartment renters. You may get some sales, but not enough to justify this market. On the other hand if you are marketing these same products to a list that has just heard a lecture on the need to grow your own food, with a good product at a reasonable cost you should expect to do well. It is in marketing to the appropriate list that the numbers will help you to be more effective.

Core Numbers in Sales

As in previously covered aspects of business, for advertising help look at the core numbers of your business chart. Each of the core numbers emphasizes a different aspect of your business. Use the numbers to achieve your specific goals. The following list is in the order of the importance of the numbers:

Integrative Vision Number – the reduced total (remember, the reduced total is derived by adding the digits of the total until you reach a single digit or a master number) of the five core numbers. The integrative vision number is the method of approach.

1- With a 1 integrative vision number approach the market with innovative ideas. Don't be easily swayed by outside influences.
2- With a 2, be non-confrontational. Negotiate to reach agreement. Relate the meeting to past activities.
3- With a 3, be a bit more conversational. Build rapport through finding common interests. An upbeat attitude and a winning smile carry the day.
4- With a 4, Be prepared with accurate facts and figures. You may not need this detail, but have it ready if the customer desires it.
5- With a 5, stay on the cutting edge. Sticking with a single method will bore you and your boredom will show. Let your personality shine through.
6- With a 6, keep a genuinely caring attitude. The warmth of your approach will determine the response.
7- With a 7, an analytic approach works best. Be prepared for some misunderstandings, so get feedback from the customer to be sure that your words were understood as you meant them.
8- With an 8, approach the situation from a base of power. A wimpy presentation will fall flat. Be careful that the power base does not disintegrate into an egotistical attitude.
9- With a 9, bring a caring attitude. Relate the product to a societal benefit. Appeal to the social instincts of your customer.
11- see the 2 entry, Emphasize creative ideas. Let your personality show through.
22- see the 4 entry. Paint a grand picture. A small vision will not sell.
33- see the 6 entry. Bring a teaching aspect into your presentation. Train your customer to see the importance of using your product.

Life Path Number – The reduced total of the digits of the birth date. This number contains the lesson to be developed in your business. It has traits that must be integrated into your advertising plan.

1- With a 1 life path number, take the initiative to connect with your customer. Use novel methods of contact.
2- With a 2, a series of contacts, preferably in writing, ads or media, usually works best.
3- With a 3, take a lighter tone. An uplifting conversation is better than a hard sell.
4- With a 4, Be business like. Excessive extraneous conversation will kill the momentum to the sale. Build a solid case.
5- With a 5, carry the day with the strength of your personality.
6- With a 6, warm up the atmosphere by tactfully asking about the customer's family, explore possible mutual acquaintances, then get down to the business at hand.
7- With a 7, bring up research studies. Comparisons are effective.

8- With an 8, take a formal approach. Dress a cut above the usual. Present an air of comfortable sophistication.
9- With a 9, appeal to the customer's desire to be a good citizen. Create an ideal vision of the use of your product or service.
11- see the 2 entry. Find the spiritual or metaphysical component of your product or service. Look beyond the strictly financial benefit.
22- see the 4 entry. Talk in expansive terms. See the big picture
33- see the 6 entry. Encourage questions about the product or service and how it fits into the total business picture. Position yourself as a knowledgeable mentor.

Expression Number –The reduced total of the values of all the letters in your business name. For numerology purposes we do not usually include designations such as inc or ltd. The expression shows talents that need to be used in your promotions.

The expression number follows the same patterns as the life path. See the above entries

Soul Urge – the total of the values of all the vowels in your business name. This number shows the motivation that must be behind your marketing.

1- With a 1 soul urge, your motivation is to work independently from your own ideas, with a view toward reaching your goals.
2- With a 2, you are willing to do whatever is necessary to get the job done without concern about getting credit for your effort.
3- With a 3, you want to make every contact fun. When the session gets too heavy, it may be desirable to postpone to another time.
4- With a 4, you will feel insecure if you have not laid out the full plan. Be careful that you do not persist past the point where the customer is ready to buy. You could kill the sale by adding more detail.
5- With a 5, your desire is to give the project a lick and a promise and get on with something else. Discipline is desirable to complete the transaction. Making the same presentation repeatedly will be boring, so vary your approach.
6- With a 6, you need some positive feedback to feel connected. Bring balance to the presentation. Let your desire to serve be evident.
7- With a 7, new knowledge is a plus. Try to gain information from your customers that will be helpful in future presentations. Observe different ways of seeing the world.
8- With an 8, sell value and quality. A discount price will get you into a downward spiral. You are the best and you want the best for your customers.
9- With a 9, reach out to people with an open hand. Be generous in your offers. Add an emotional appeal in your presentation.

With an 11, see the 2 entry. Work from an enlightened base. Be sure that your offers are good for everyone involved.

With a 22, see the 4 entry. Create a challenge that may be difficult to reach, but that gets the adrenaline flowing.

With a 33, see the 6 entry. Bring usable content to your presentations. Even if the customer does not immediately buy, leave him with something to think about.

Personality – the reduced total of the consonants in your business name. This number designates how your market will perceive your business. It is the first impression of people unfamiliar with your business.

1- With a 1 personality, the business is perceived as innovative and independent.
2- With a 2, the perception is a soft touch. People will expect answers to all their questions. The image is warm and sensitive sophistication.
3- With a 3, the image is chatty and friendly. Expect to attract time wasters.
4- With a 4, the perception is hard working, dependable and financially solid.
5- With a 5, the image is of constant change. It will attract those seeking cutting edge products and ideas.
6- With a 6, the image is of good taste, caring and responsibility.
7- With a 7, there is a perception of aloofness. The business will be perceived as different and maybe a bit eccentric.
8- With an 8, the perception will be a take charge business. It can be intimidating to less confident people. The 8 lends the perception of a large operation even for a one man show.
9- With a 9, the perception is approachable, generous and warm. Expect solicitations for public causes.

-With an 11, see the 2 entry. The perception is a business with keen insight into the higher realm. It is great for metaphysical work, public speaking and motivational materials.
-With a 22, see the 4 entry. The perception is of a business that will become great. The potential is evident.
-With a 33, the perception is of loving sharing of knowledge. It is a teaching energy.

Birth Day - The reduced total of the founding day number. This number reveals some obvious traits that are readily apparent to your customers. Don't try to hide these characteristics, but capitalize on them in your ad copy.

1- independence, high achiever.
2- sensitive, peacemaker, coordinator.
3- communicator, life of the party, spendthrift.
4- hard working, persistent, stubborn, frugal.
5- easily bored, flitting, discontent, loves travel and change.
6- nurturing, good business base, good taste, friendly.
7- aloof, analytical, knowledgeable, different, intuitive.
8- big thinking, quality conscious, elegant, demanding.
9- philanthropic, idealistic, emotional, society leader.
11- intuitive, inner strength.
22- business builder, grand plans, coordinator.
33- healing touch, acting and singing talents.

Best Approach to Customers

In addition to the viewpoint from your business perspective, also consider the best approach to each customer. Use the quick check from chapter 9 on first impressions. Work with the first name of the person with whom you are dealing. Since the vowels are stronger than the consonants, read the vowel first and if there is a consonant in front of the vowel, read the first consonant as a modifier.

Vowel Approaches

- A=1. Present the idea so that he thinks it is his initiative to purchase
- E=5. Avoid too much detail. Look for quick buying signs and write up the order as soon as you get a positive go ahead.
- I=9. Appeal to his altruism. Show how the purchase will help him to benefit the broader society.
- O=6. Appeal to his love of home and family
- U=3. Don't burden the presentation with a lot of detail unless requested. Expect a quick decision.
- Y=7. Be sure the customer has plenty of time and detail for a full analysis. Don't interrupt the process by talking through his contemplations.
- W=5. Show the innovative features. Appeal to his need for the latest version of the product. He will want to be the first to have the item.

Consonants Approaches

Take the value of the consonants from the conversion table and the traits from the number meanings. Modify the vowel meaning to adjust for the consonant.

Example 1: If you are making a presentation to William, the first vowel is I (9). The approach is to appeal to his altruistic side. The first consonant is W (5) He does not want an in depth presentation. You will lose him with too much detail. Make a quick emotional appeal and ask for the decision.

Example 2: Mary has a first vowel of A (1) and a first consonant of M (4). Give her the facts and figures. Let her digest the information and come to her own conclusion. She will tell you why she decided to buy or pass. If she is undecided, probe to be sure she has considered all aspects.

The first part of this chapter pertains to your promotional copy and indirect marketing. The quick check applies in any face to face or telephone contact.

Chapter 21

Sales Management

Advertising is an essential part of doing business, but it is not always clear what ads will be effective. Selling is an art. Although there are studies to show best methods, you cannot be sure how the market will respond. If you are tracking your results and testing your campaigns, you may have a reasonable idea what sales you will make. You can only arrive at that position through regular promotions that provide averages.

Other considerations can skew your results. Are you tapping a new market? Has the general economy changed? Is your product or service becoming obsolete through advances in technology? Is the market saturated? Do you have additional products to sell to your customers? Any of these factors can change your results.

Until your business reaches a break point, you are probably doing all the promotion and sales yourself. The numbers from your charts give guidance as to your best approach. Some businesses will do well with direct calls or face to face presentations. Others need to work behind the scenes in direct mail or internet marketing. You may have a mix of numbers that suggests a combination of methods.

In this information age, so much material is available. Just starting out, this overload of ideas can sink your business. Every time you pull up your e-mails or surf the web, there is another must have e-book or program. You can get bogged down in trying to implement several at the same time. Remember, this great must-have idea will either still be around when you are ready to add another step or it will have become passé. Either way, keep your focus to grow your business through an orderly process. Pursuit of every new sure idea probably has been the main reason for business failure or working long hours with limited income.

Many marketing systems have come and gone. Those who develop them may give their projects a major launch with prominent marketers as JV partners. It makes a big splash. A lot of money is brought in. Everybody gets on the band wagon and promotes this plan as the ultimate breakthrough. You get e-mails *ad nauseum* for the pre-launch, the launch and the post launch. The next month, a new program is touted. Try to find a follow-up success rate for the long term on any of these plans. It will be difficult. Most of the money made through these programs is from selling the program itself rather than by using the program to develop your business. Don't become a program junkie, unless that is the focus of your business.

Some of these systems are successful until too many people try to use them. Then they become stale and a replacement comes along. If you jump on each new plan, you will spend a lot more money than you take in. Each program has a learning curve. It takes time to institute a system. You must either delay the new purchase or discard what you spent time and money putting together last week. Read the stories of top marketers. Many have spent $50,000, $100,000 dollars and more before they found the appropriate program and system for them.

Choose a method that matches your Integrative vision number and stick with it until you have mastered it. Once you fully know the system, you can evaluate whether it is the right direction for your business. You will be lured by several sure-fire methods that can't possibly lose. The new system promises instant wealth beyond your wildest dreams. Many of the marketers of these systems have yet to make any substantial amount by following the plan they are touting. Do you want to be a constant beta tester or do you want to build a solid business?

The above scenario does not apply to a valid coaching or mentoring program. The difference is that a coach will tailor the package for your business to take you quickly to profit. It is the age-old dichotomy – do you have more time or more money to grow your business. Find the right balance for you.

Many very successful internet businesses operate without employees. There is an ego satisfaction of being the owner of a business that employs a lot of people. My rule of thumb is that employees are a last resort after you have exhausted all other methods, such as outsourcing, joint ventures and cooperative projects.

As with several of the past lessons, keep in mind the order of strength of the numbers in your chart. The stronger numbers take priority. Use the weaker numbers as modifiers to add a nuance. For example, if your life path number is a 6, which emphasizes service and caring, and your personality number is a 1, which emphasizes independence and goal oriented practices, your advertising would stress the service elements, with a soft sell mention of your discount pricing.

The priority of the chart numbers is integrative vision, life path, expression, soul urge, personality and birth day. See the Appendix for a reference on the meanings and chapter 4 for the calculations.

The numbers fall into related groupings:

1, 4, 8, are business oriented practical numbers. With these numbers your advertising should emphasize good business practices. You can create credibility by touting the length of time you have successfully operated the business (the longer the better), the competitive advantage of buying from you, and value for the cost. These numbers can be confrontational. Show confidence, but be careful that your tone does not become arrogant. Honesty is essential in your promotions. Hype that cannot be proven will bring about a disconnect of the business from your customers.

This triad works well for major corporations, entrepreneurs, business coaches and retail outlets.

2, 6, 9, are customer related numbers. They are warm and nurturing energies. The advertising should be written from the customer's viewpoint. Show your service policy. Your caring should be evident.

This triad works well for medical care facilities, schools, philanthropic organizations and counselors.

3 and 5 are sales numbers. Your advertising needs to be persuasive. Innovative ideas and unusual applications of your products would be well-received. These numbers are most effective in direct contact with the customer either by telephone or in person.

This set of numbers works well in direct marketing to the consumer.

7 stands alone. The energy of the 7 makes it a bit aloof. It looks at the world from a different viewpoint. As a result, the advertising from the 7 is often misunderstood. If you are advertising from this energy, be sure that you get feedback from disinterested parties to be sure the copy says what you meant it to say. 7 is generally not a prime business energy, but it can work well for a technical or research oriented business. Because 7 has a strong inclination to ponder the deeper questions of life and the universe, it is also a strong number for metaphysical endeavors.

This number works well for laboratories, metaphysical businesses, research facilities and university research departments.

The master numbers – 11/2, 22/4 and 33/6 – follow the reduced numbers, but with greater intensity.

To determine the approach, follow the integrative vision number. To determine the marketing goal, follow the life path number.

To determine content, follow the expression number

To determine the underlying motivation, follow the soul urge number. To determine the first impression, follow the personality number.

If these numbers are coordinated harmoniously, you will be able to develop a consistent marketing message. If there is discord in the numbers, you need to follow the priorities – stronger numbers modified by the weaker numbers.

To fully use this information requires a working knowledge of the number meanings and the comparisons of the numbers.

Chapter 22

Clients

This Chapter discusses client relationships. Although there are standard principles in developing good client relationships, by looking at the numbers, you gain insight into how different dominant numbers create unique benefits from certain methods.

Solid business practices are not eliminated by the numbers, but in every aspect of the business you have choices within the set parameters. You, no doubt, have heard *ad nauseum*, that to be successful in business you must build relationships with your customers. That adage is still true, but the ways of maintaining this relationship are changing with new means of communication. In the small town restaurant on the square or the Wild West Saloon, or any business where you are the sole source of a desirable product, the customers come to you in a face to face meeting.

In a more remote marketplace, where your customers can be spread around the world, this intimate type of relationship is not possible. You need to create the sense of relationship with people whom you have not met, and likely may never meet. The type of business that you are running will dictate some ways to create the feeling of connection. Customer relations overlap the advertising approach. Much of the material of the prior two chapters can also apply here.

Customers are the life blood of any business. Without buyers, your products are worthless. They earn you nothing sitting on your warehouse shelves. The lessons in advertising dealt with bringing new customers to your business. Keeping these customers coming back for more of your offerings determines your business success and is the thrust of this chapter. The initial contact and sale is a test run of your integrity and the quality of your product or services. It is likely to be a relatively minor sale. If you are continuously selling an entry level product, you will work very hard for a limited income.

Your customer relations approach will determine if this customer will return for a more substantial investment in what you offer. Ideally, you want to provide an outstanding offering that not only will get repeated purchases, but will provide incentive for those customers to promote you through word of mouth.

This chapter applies the core numbers of your business chart to your customer relations. As before, use the priority of strength of the core numbers to determine your starting point for evaluating customer maintenance.

Prior chapters looked at reaching customers through advertising from the viewpoint of what to offer and the content of the promotion. This lesson evaluates the style of customer relations from what the business demands. It is how you connect with customers to create rapport and credibility.

Each number has distinctive traits that may or may not be similar to those of other numbers. Giving equal weight to all the core numbers will put you in a bind. How would you resolve conflicting energies? The weaker numbers modify the stronger numbers. For example, if you have a 5 life path and a 4 personality, the life path is stronger than the personality, so you would start from the 5 – an active, risk taking number– and showing that the impulsiveness of the 5 is modified by the stability of the 4. The approach is to move forward in unusual ways, but only with a firm financial footing. The underlying 4 would keep the dominant 5 from acting too speculatively, but would not be strong enough to unduly limit the 5.

Customer Relations Approach for Each Number

- 1 will keep customers coming back for more when you present new ideas and stimulating products. With a strong 1, you have a chance to tout your company. Mention your accomplishments without arrogance or condescension. Don't be shy about letting your customers know who you are.
- 2- With a strong 2, your approach needs to be understated. Negotiation will get you further than confrontation. An historical perspective showing stability and credibility will serve you well. A well-reasoned presentation is more effective than hype.
- 3 requires a lighter approach. A bit of social chit-chat is desirable. Even in written communication, personal tidbits can work well. Appropriate humor can be effective.
- 4 requires a strict business approach. Facts and figures are important. Avoid flashy presentations. Be straightforward in making claims. Proof of your position is vital. Honesty must be a watchword, both overtly and in omissions.
- 5 emphasizes constant change. You need to be flexible and responsive. You could develop a whole tool chest of approaches that can be interspersed to provide interest. Taking the show on the road would suit you fine.
- 6 is the number of balance. It is warm and loving with a solid sense of good business practices. Create a homey atmosphere in the office. Ads with a mixture of song and dance would be appealing. It is important with this energy to build a solid connection with customers.
- 7 is aloof. It is marked by a lack of emotional display. With a strong 7 consider most of your communication to be in written form. Problem solving is a forte of the 7. Find ways to connect in areas that need solutions, such as software programs that handle difficult challenges with ease. This number does not lend itself well to outside sales people.

- With a strong 8, your business needs to stay at the top of its game. It needs to be the model of integrity and strength. Image is important. Create a feeling within your customers that they are dealing with a top-notch company on all levels.
- 9 This number requires a societal element. If the company or product is not obviously designed to improve society, create the perception that dealing with you will enhance the planet. This number should never be caught polluting the environment or raising animals in a cruel manner for food. The company must take responsibility for any harm done to the users.
- 11 This master number requires an enlightened business approach. The company philosophy will be scrutinized. Much of the decision making will be intuitive. Seek to connect with clients from a soul level.
- 22 Because the 22 demands a grand vision, the plans and structure of the business must support major projects. Create an image of greatness. Build excitement in clients and investors for ventures that go beyond their current thinking. Let your customers see the grand design and provide a means for them to be a part of it.
- 33 The 33 reaches out to the customer base with a teaching approach. Persuade your customers by showing the details that go into your product or service. Even if your methods are the same as everyone else in the industry, by spelling out the steps in the creation of the product, you gain an edge over those companies that follow the same procedures, but fail to disclose the process to their customers. It will seem that you are doing something unique. Later disclosures by competitors will seem like a copycat application.

An Example of How the Approach is Developed

I have taken the numbers from an actual chart, but not one previously involved in this study. This chart shows a difficult business approach because of the conflicting numbers and a lot of non-businesslike energy.

    Integrative Vision = 5
    Life Path = 9
    Expression = 7
    Soul urge = 1
    Personality = 6
    Birthday = 9

The numbers are listed in the order of strength. I will first set out each of the energies separately and show how they are synthesized.

> 5 – (integrative vision) The 5 emphasizes constant change. You need to be flexible and responsive. You could develop a whole tool chest of approaches that can be interspersed to provide interest. Taking the show on the road would suit you fine.

> 9 – (Life path) The 9 requires a societal element. If the company or product is not obviously designed to improve society, create the perception that dealing with you will enhance the planet. This number should never be caught polluting

the environment or raising animals in a cruel manner for food. The company must take responsibility for any harm done to the users.

7 – (Expression) The 7 is aloof. It is marked by a lack of emotional display. With a strong 7 consider most of your communication to be in written form. Problem solving is a forte of the 7. Find ways to connect in areas that need solutions, such as with software programs that handle difficult challenges with ease. This number does not lend itself well to outside sales people.

1 – (Soul urge) The 1 will keep customers coming back for more when you present new ideas and stimulating products. With a strong 1, you have a chance to tout your company. Mention your accomplishments without arrogance or condescension. Don't be shy about letting your customers know who you are.

6 – (Personality) The 6 is the number of balance. It is warm and loving with a solid sense of good business practices. Create a homey atmosphere in the office. Ads with a mixture of song and dance would be appealing. It is important with this energy to build a solid relationship with customers.

This set of core numbers is not especially good business energy and contains a number of conflicts. I have chosen this chart to show how even with opposite extremes, you can reach a compromise.

My Thinking in Setting Up the Approach

Start with the Integrative Vision. It is the designation of the usual approach of the business. This chart has a 5, which shows a need for flexibility and variety.

The life path and expression are of about equal value. We have a 9 life path and a 7 expression. We add a societal emphasis and an analytical component. The 9 has a compassion for society as a whole and an idealized view of what can be accomplished. The company promotes itself through appropriate charitable giving. The 7 hides the emotion of the 9, but does not eliminate it.

We now have a flexible approach without a set pattern that has a well thought out emphasis upon the benefits to society of the product or services of the company that are promoted through appropriate charitable giving. These benefits are presented with limited emotion.

The soul urge is a 1. This company desires to work from an independent base in order to incorporate innovative ideas. The 1 shares the independence of the 5 and fits into the pattern comfortably.

We now have a flexible approach without a set pattern that has a well thought out emphasis upon the benefits to society of the product or services of the company that are promoted through appropriate charitable giving. These benefits are presented with limited emotion. The approach will be unique because of the specific business ideas of the company.

The 6 personality relates to the 9, but on a more personal basis. It requires a nurturing attitude. It emphasizes a family feeling that is lacking in the other core numbers. It is the lesser energy, so we will add an element of care without making it the dominant approach.

We can ignore the 9 birth day since it reinforces the 9 life path.

The Final Statement of Approach
This business takes a flexible approach without a set pattern that has a well thought out emphasis upon the benefits to society of the product or services of the company that are promoted through appropriate charitable giving. These benefits are presented with limited emotion. The approach will be unique because of the specific business ideas of the company. Customer support is expressed positively, but without undue emphasis.

Chapter 23

Financial

Chapter 13 dealt with financing for start-up or expansion. This chapter discusses handling of operational finances. Each number emphasizes a distinct approach to money. Keeping of accurate records is vital to a successful business. Some numbers revel in setting up the books and making sure that they are always in balance. Other numbers consider a lick and a promise adequate. As mentioned in other lessons, when your business numbers leave a gap in a vital function, you may want to outsource the project or hire someone who has the inclination for the job.

Long range planning requires that you know what activities are profitable. Your business may need to engage in certain activities that are not profitable *per se*, but that contribute to the overall picture. Be careful that such projects do not consume an undue percentage of your staff time.

Assessing Your Business Risk Comfort Level

Assess your business risk comfort level. The numbers of the core will help to delineate where you can function. Too much risk can lead to sleepless nights. When the business is too cautious, it can stagnate or become unprofitable.

Start by considering the mix of the business core numbers in order of strength. By now, you should be familiar with your core numbers. (That order, again, is integrative vision, life path, expression, soul urge, personality and birth day.) Most likely you have some conflicts and inconsistencies in the chart. Too much energy devoted to a single number or grouping of numbers can be unbalanced, so conflict is not necessarily negative. Within each group, the individual numbers have distinct characteristics as well.

Similar Number Groupings

    1, 4, 8 – these are practical business oriented numbers, with little desire for risk. A solid financial base is required

    3, 6, 9 – these are creative numbers, often impractical about money

2, 6, 9 – replacing the 3 energy with the 2 adds a practical sense to the triad. This triad provides a nice balance between risk and stability.

3, 5 – These numbers are likely to go overboard on the side of risk

7 is aloof from the other numbers. Money is not a big issue.

Use the **example** from the last chapter to show risk taking conflict:

> Integrative Vision = 5
> Life Path = 9
> Expression = 7
> Soul urge = 1
> Personality=6
> Birthday = 9

With a 5 integrative vision number, this business is likely to be impulsive in jumping into new ventures. It is comfortable in following an intuitive approach to the next project (9 and 7 energy) with a minimum of due diligence. With a 7 expression, there is a perception that whatever problems arise can be solved in process and that the money will be there when it is needed. The 9 life path and birth day justify the risk if there is a strong benefit to society from the plan. The 1 soul urge will support the project if it uses innovative thinking. 1 will be less enthusiastic if a similar project has been done before. The 6 personality adds some limited sense of responsibility to ideas that are too far out.

Record Keeping

2, 4 and 6 are detail oriented enough to handle the bookkeeping. Accuracy is important. These numbers are not prominent in our example business. The records are likely to often be in shambles. The business should consider outsourcing or hiring someone to do this job. Even with a solid 2 record keeper, this business will have a continuing struggle keeping up to date. The lax atmosphere will create a tendency to ignore the importance of the data. The record keeper must be a strong enough personality to demand that the data submission be accurate and timely. It will be a constant battle that will wear down even a strong person. Because the 2 doesn't like confrontation, 4 energy may be required.

Some of the other energies may be better able to bridge the gap between the need for good records and the tendency of the business to ignore this vital function.

1- 1 would rather delegate this job. 1 does not like the confinement of this much detail.
2- a superb record keeper. 2 will work with the figures to be sure there is no discrepancy or omission.
3- Keep the 3 as far away from the books as possible. 3 is often illogical about money. A lick and a promise is acceptable. Spending is desired.
4- A solid financial energy. 4 prefers large reserves and a well thought out plan for any spending.
5- Has the ability to bring in money easily, so often holds proper records in disdain.
6- Brings a comfortable balance between the creative needs of the business and a solid base.

7- Would rather not be bothered. It can be detail oriented on its own research, but sees the financial records as a necessary nuisance.
8- Has the ability to handle the records well, but would constantly feel that it is a waste of his or her time. The 8 is the manager and policy maker.
9- Often has issues about money. His generous nature may question a more rigorous business use that could create emotional conflicts.

Master numbers – since record keeping is done at the mundane level, master numbers should be read as the reduced number.

Long Term Financial Planning

Each business will have a natural level for long term planning. For our sample business, very little consideration will go into the long term. It uses a "take each day as it comes" approach, with a vision of where it wants to be down the road. The step by step plan will feel confining.

Other businesses will not move forward without knowing the end from the beginning. These are the opposite extremes. Most companies will be somewhere in between - reasonably detailed planning with enough flexibility to adjust to the daily vicissitudes. In some instances, new ideas may bring this company to a different course.

In all cases, the long term planning decisions require knowing where you are at the moment. That knowledge comes from good records. It is not enough to think that you are aware of the cash flow and financial availability merely from your knowledge of the business. Without adequate records, you may have some unpleasant surprises. It may seem as though a lot of money is coming in. It may seem that it is sufficient to do the next step. Your mind can play tricks on you. Get it down in concrete form where you can look at the full picture to avoid coming up short.

In addition, you cannot set and track your goals from memory. Proper records also encourage you to put in that extra bit of effort when you are falling short. It can mean the difference between success and failure. Good management is based upon accurate data. Poor management is a leading cause of business failure. Give your business the chance to succeed.

For Long Term Planning

>The **soul urge** number determines the comfort level
>The **expression** shows the ability to handle the details
>The **integrative vision** number shows how the business involves others
>The **personality** shows how others perceive the business

The **life path** shows an umbrella energy that over shadows the other numbers

1. is constantly coming up with new ideas. A long term plan must be general without too much restriction.
2. is uncomfortable without every detail in place. It will see the historical perspective as well as the future plan. Nothing is left to chance.

3. is likely to wing it. Any plan will be restricting. 3 knows that it can talk its way out of almost any difficulty it encounters.
4. is a solid, but not exciting, financial planner. The first consideration will be how to pay for it. The detailed plan must project conservative earnings and costs. 4 does not like surprises, particularly in finances.
5. has the ability to bring in money easily. Planning is not a priority. It takes discipline for 5 to either do the record keeping or to even cooperate with someone else doing it.
6. maintains a nice balance between the extremes. It needs the assurance of a detailed plan with a regular review of the progress.
7. can plan a project to death. Every piece is analyzed, often to the extent of discouragement
8. takes responsibility for executing the plan. It can see the total picture clearly and see what needs to be included in the plan. Most likely the 8 will delegate the creation of the plan, subject to his review.
9. is a perfectionist. It wants a perfect plan and perfect execution. The 9 tends to constantly tweak the plan, which could leave less energy for implementation.

Working with your own business chart, the above list gives you a default position. In your business planning, certain principles must be followed for business success. If your primary numbers do not support these principles, determine to bring in people or services to fill the gap. Then allow these people to do the job.

Chapter 24

Plan

This chapter pulls together the elements discussed in the prior material. Choose a chart to follow. The chart can be a business you already have up and running, one you anticipate establishing or just one you are using for an example. Trying to follow this material without a specific chart in front of you, will allow you to miss important details. Once you have put this information together in one chart, you can more easily follow the same procedure for any chart.

The business plan presented here could probably better be named a business blueprint. It sets a structure for establishing and operating your business. It is not a plan that you take to the bank for financing. That type of business plan looks more specifically at the qualifications of management, the results of the marketing and the financial projections of the business. The bank wants to know whether the business is solid enough to make it a loan. This plan will help you to build a solid business.

This chapter and the next is a case study on Life Path Numerology Center, Inc. In this chapter, I discuss the thinking that went into developing the plan. The following chapter shows the actual plan.

The Elements of the Plan

The Business and Personal Charts

Prepare a chart for the business, your own personal chart and a personal chart for your key people. Compare the personal year cycles for compatibility. Anyone who is in an incompatible cycle, particularly adjacent to the business cycle (3&4, 4&5, etc,) is likely to experience burn-out. Using the reference, get a sense of the characteristics of each person compared to the business.

The Founding Date
The date the business was established determines the business cycles. It determines several of the core numbers. In the case study of the next two lessons you will clearly see how to tweak the start date for the numbers you want.

Business Name
There are both number results and marketing considerations in choosing an appropriate name. The name should be reasonably short or descriptive to be easily remembered. You will write it often, so don't overburden yourself unnecessarily. The name should lend itself to branding. Some business names were simply made up, but have taken on a generic overtone such as Kleenex, Xerox, Scotch Tape, Post-it Notes.

Legal Format
It is important to look down the road when you are creating your business to determine whether a corporation, an LLC, an unincorporated proprietorship or a partnership is best. By setting up the business for future needs, you avoid disruptive redoing of the legalities.

Purpose
The life path number shows the purpose that the business must strive to reach. Fulfilling this purpose will propel the business to success. This number in conjunction with the rest of the core also shows the abundance or lack of opportunities.

Motivation
The soul urge number shows an element that must be fulfilled in the operation of the business. If the needs of this number are ignored, no matter how successful the business becomes, it will not seem to be enough.

Needed Talents
The expression number shows the supportive talents that must be in the mix of officers and employees in the business. These talents will move the company toward the goal set by the life path number.

First Impressions
The personality number gives a glimpse of the public image. It is the view that strangers not otherwise familiar with the business will have. This view will likely be modified as an individual deals with the business.

Action Method
The integrative vision number shows the natural approach to the operation of the business. Using the approach designated by the integrative vision numbers will follow the natural rhythm of your business.

Business Image
Creating an image statement will help your business to send out a consistent character. Customers will know what to expect and your staff will have a solid guideline for their actions.

Preferences
Coordinating the preferences questionnaire and the core numbers of your charts will provide a guide for the office atmosphere. The preferences complement the image statement.

Planning for Expansion
Consider your goal for the ultimate size of the business in the initial planning stages. It is likely that your early vision will need to be expanded later as your comfort zone grows, but looking at growth possibilities from the start allows the mechanisms for expansion to be incorporated into the business without disruption when the growth happens.

Vision
The vision statement and the mission statement are the bedrock for the operation of your business. They are a statement of how you relate to your customer base.

Style
Style relates back to your preferences. It covers more detail in the actual setup of your office.

Hiring
By the time you are ready to add staff, many of the other elements will be in place. Prospective employees will evaluate the physical elements as well as the atmosphere created by these elements, to determine if they are a good fit. You will evaluate the fit from their numbers.

Personnel Placement
Some employees may be a good fit for the job, but not a match to the business numbers. Be careful about hiring this person. There is a danger of quick burn-out. Other employees may be a good fit for the company, but not for the job or the nature of the work. They could be an excellent choice if you have another position available that matches his or her numbers.

Vendors
A match in the numbers creates long term relationship potential. Obtaining data to run the numbers can be difficult. You probably will go through the process only for major suppliers where a relationship is established. You likely will not need to go to this effort for small purchases.

Distributors
Be more careful with distributors. To some extent they represent your business to their base. The reputation of the distributor can come back to you.

Sales
The numbers of your charts will clue you in to how best to market your products or services. A sales staff requires certain skills that may vary with the nature of the business.

Sales Management
When you grow to the level of requiring a sales manager, it is not always appropriate to promote your top producer. The necessary skills for sales and management are different. With the numbers, the manager can know just how to motivate each *rep*.

Clients
The numbers can give you an edge in knowing how that client wants to be perceived. With a quick check you have a clue for building immediate rapport.

Finances
Good record keeping is the lifeblood of your business. Without an accurate picture of your progress you will make inappropriate decisions.

Steps to Create the Business Plan

The dilemma stems from your eagerness to get going and the time required for this planning. By doing these steps in advance, you run less risk of having to redo some aspects of your business. On the other hand you can plan your business to death and never get it going. Find the proper balance for you.

For an established business, you may find conflicts or desired changes. By running the numbers you may discover where some of the snags are and why your business may have problems.

In numerology, there is no perfect chart or perfect plan. The chart is interdependent. When you tweak one number, it changes other parts of the chart. Your goal is to get the most workable chart for you.

The starting point for the other steps is your personal chart.

Choose the appropriate legal format. This choice will determine any other charts that must be considered. Determine whether you will be the primary manager of the business. For a partnership, run the personal chart of all partners. Determine the coordination of the numbers from each chart. Be sure that the personal year cycles are compatible.

Set the business cycles to match the primary decision maker. This coordination will determine the desired founding date. For a sole proprietorship or a corporation where you are the primary decision maker, try to place the business on your personal cycle to avoid conflict.

The start date determines the life path number. From Chapter 6, determine if that number is acceptable. If not, you may need to wait until next year or change the cycle.

Choose the business name. This name will set the interior core numbers. Tweak the name to give a desirable set of numbers.

Create the business chart from the name and founding date. Compare the business chart with your personal chart for compatibility. Evaluate each of the core numbers by reading each of the core number meanings.

The integrative vision number is found by adding together the five core numbers, life path, expression, soul urge, personality and birth day. Develop a business approach based upon the integrative vision number.

Create the image statement.

Bring in your personal preferences.

Bring in your vision of how large you wish the business to grow. Determine whether the numbers support that level. Go beyond your present comfort zone. If you are following these steps, the potential may surprise you.

Create your vision statement and mission statement.

Create an office plan including business address, telephone number, color scheme, furnishings and organization. You may not be able to implement this plan immediately, but creating it will draw it to you.

The Operation of the Business

Employee and Staff

Determine which prospects are a good fit for your business and the job opening.

Determine proper employee placement for the greatest production, job satisfaction and stability in the workforce.

Vendors and Distributors

Evaluate your long-term vendors.

Choose your distributors.

Sales

Consider your best sales approach and marketing measures. Determine who can best fit this approach.

Determine how to control the sales process, including management and the motivation of your sales staff.

Client and Customer Relations

Set up your procedures for building relationships with clients.

Finances

Set up your books and procedures. Determine what records need to be kept. This list can vary by type of business. Be sure that the person responsible for the daily entries has numbers that show attention to detail.

Chapter 25

Case Study Part 1

This chapter and the next take you through the elements of the book by using Life Path Numerology Center, Inc. as a study example. In this lesson, I will let you in on my thinking process to determine the application of the numbers to our own business.

The next chapter will show the completed business plan.

Life Path Numerology Center was originally incorporated on October 22, 1996. The Center has developed differently from our initial concept. Some of the starting founders are no longer in the business. As it became more my operation, with less input from others, having the business on a cycle that was compatible, but different from mine began to create conflicts in certain years. In developing this material, I determined that it was desirable to reincorporate. The new incorporation date puts the business on the same cycle as my personal cycle. Since the new filing date on December 23, 2009, the monthly income for the business has doubled. By eliminating the conflicting personal years, the work moves more freely.

With a re-incorporation, the choice was whether to keep the same name or to work out a new name. We tried tweaking the name to improve the numbers, but the old name was too established. Any more desirable names were too far off the original. A change would not have been beneficial enough to counterbalance the negatives of a change.

Over the years, the business became a *de facto* sole proprietorship. The corporate form has been dropped without the necessity of revamping the numbers.

The current chart may seem to violate some of the rules from the lessons. If we were starting from scratch, the chart may be different. You can see the difference by comparing the new chart with the previous chart. Early on in the course, I suggested that for an already established business a bit of tweaking to modify the most difficult challenges may be better than going back to square one and starting over.

You will never get a perfect chart. All of the core numbers are interdependent. Changing one will modify others. The goal is to get as workable a chart as possible with coordination between the business chart and your personal chart. When there are several key players in the business, the situation becomes more complex, because you will want as close a co-ordination between the business chart, the personal charts with the business and the personal charts with each other.

The smoothest co-ordination for the business is produced when the business chart is a good match for the primary decision maker. Usually, a chart compatible to the primary leader will work with the other key players as well. If someone involved has major conflicts with the business chart, particularly in the personal year cycle, that person is likely to burn out or become a disruptive influence. Evaluate closely whether that person should be a part of the business, or in what capacity he or she will best fit.

Specific Comparisons for the Example Business

Original Data:

Business Name: Life Path Numerology Center, Inc. Founding date: October 22, 1996

Reincorporation Data

Business Name: Life Path Numerology Center, Inc. Founding date: December 23, 2009

	Original	Re-incorporation	My Personal Data
Life Path	(12)3	19/1	13/4
Expression	(26)8	(26)8	19/1
Soul Urge	16/7	16/7	9
Personality	19/1	19/1	19/1
Founding Day	22/4	(23)5	(30)3
Integrative Vision	(41)5	22/4	(18)9
2018 Personal year	16/7	19/1	19/1

Evaluation of the Changes

Personal Year Cycles: A major need was to bring the business cycle to the same as my personal cycle. We accomplished this goal. The re-incorporation had to be done in 2009. The only remaining day available was December 23. Waiting until 2010 would have created a 2 life path, which we did not want. With the revamped founding date, we lost the benefit of 2010 being an 8 personal year. The 8 is usually a very productive energy. However, my 2 personal year would have worked against the strong ambition of the 8 to create a negative conflict.

Name: Because the name was well established and with some branding, it seemed to be undesirable to change the name of the business. We could not find a good tweak that gave any advantage. As a result, the interior numbers are unchanged from the original chart to the reincorporated chart.

Both in the original chart and the current chart, there is an inherent conflict between the 7 soul urge and the 8 expression. We accepted this challenge because the 7 works well for metaphysical pursuits. It provides a depth of study which we desired in breaking new ground in numerology. The 8 expression gives the level of management and money oriented talents to bring success to the business. Since 7 is the soul urge, money is not the primary motivation for the work of the Center. This orientation suits my personal 9 soul urge and 9 integrative vision. Based upon the strength of the core numbers, the expression takes precedence over the soul urge.

The 8 expression co-ordinates well with the 1 life path and the 22/4 integrative vision to provide a solid base.

Life Path: the change is from a 3 to a 1. 1 is a practical business energy that promotes creative ideas. The 3 provided a skill with words that was desirable, but a similar energy is brought into the chart through the 5 founding day. The 3 was in conflict with my personal life path, but matched my 3 birth day.

By reducing the life path from a 3 to a 1, it further limits the available opportunities by 2 places. During the existence of the Center, we have pioneered areas where we had to create our own opportunities, so this downshift should not be a major factor.

Integrative Vision: The original chart had a 5 integrative vision number, which was in conflict with my 4 life path. The current 22/4 matches my personal 4 life path and raises it to a master level. This change should open up new levels of accomplishment.

Summary: When the charts show interlocking numbers in the major core numbers, it creates a solid bond. This connection is shown in the 19/1 life path of the business with the 19/1 of my personal expression. It is also enhanced with the 22/4 integrative vision of the business and my personal 13/4 life path. Getting the business on my personal cycle is a major improvement. Eliminating some of the most difficult conflicts will help. In just 2 months, I am noticing a sense of coordinated effort. It no longer feels like I am fighting the business.

Chapter 26

Case Study Part 2

When I first proposed to use Life Path Numerology Center, Inc as a case study, I had no idea that I would feel so vulnerable with the disclosure of the plan. I hope that our disclosure helps you to put together your own plan in a way that is useful in promoting your business.

Preparing the Plan

Chart Set-up
See Sample Appendix A

Integrative Vision	22/4
Life Path	19/1
Expression	26/8
Soul Urge	16/7
Personality	19/1
Founding Day	23/5

This business was re-incorporated on December 23, 2009, for the primary purpose of placing Life Path Numerology Center, Inc. on the same cycle as the primary decision maker, Daniel R. Hardt.

Name Choice
The name was not changed in the re-incorporation, because it had been well established over an active period of 13 years. The name numbers have some negative elements, but to change them would have not given a more desirable set of numbers. It was determined that we could accommodate the discord for the gains.

Legal Format

The business is a C corporation, rather than an LLC or a subchapter S. The format is also a carryover from the prior set-up, which has served us well and is desirable for expansion plans.

Purpose

The life path number which designates the purpose is a 19/1. This number indicates that the business needs to act independently, often against established ideas in marketing.

Motivation

With a 7 Soul Urge the motivation is in research areas, bringing new insights into the understanding and practice of numerology.

First Impression

A 19/1 personality requires making the pioneering spirit obvious to the general market. With the match to the Life Path, this first impression is not a façade, but an integral part of the energies of the business.

Advertising

The emphasis must be practical. The core numbers are basically business oriented. Showing how much we care, even though customer service is important to us, does not ring true in advertising. Touting a caring attitude would come across as hype.

Employees, Vendors and Distributors

Consideration of our dealings with each of these categories is on an individual basis. As a result, it has not been included in the Business Plan.

Approach to Business

The 22/4 integrative vision number requires that the thinking on every aspect of the business must be on a large scale. If the ideas are too small, the business will struggle. Grand thinking will attract the people and resources needed to accomplish the vision. Small thinking will not have the power to excite the support of those who should be involved.

Obvious Traits

The 5 founding day adds just enough 5 energy along with the six 5s in the letters of the name to allow change to occur naturally without a total disruption. Change will be constant, but within an established framework.

Business Plan for Life Path Numerology Center, Inc.

Mission Statement

The mission of Life Path Numerology Center, Inc. is to encourage the use of numerology for personal growth and business development through teaching, research, readings and product creation; to expand the market through effective outreach and to provide skilled numerologists through professional training and certification.

Vision Statement

Life Path Numerology Center, Inc. is a pioneer (19/1 life path number) in expanding the use of numerology as a business power tool. Its vision is to be a primary source of training professionals and filling the needs of the business community. It is the premier organization for setting the standards for the practice of numerology and the certification of numerologists to service this growing market. It is on the cutting edge of bringing numerology to the mainstream community. In addition, the personal growth division raises personal consultation to a higher level through requiring an above average expertise in delineating and presenting the information developed through the numbers of a chart. The work of the Center reaches and positively influences large numbers of people to improve the quality of their lives. The research of the Center (16/7 soul urge) explores areas of disagreement among numerologists and provides the depth of study to provide accurate and clear answers.

Corporate History

Life Path Numerology Center, Inc. was first incorporated on October 22, 1996, with a five member board consisting of Daniel Hardt, Timothy Phipps, Donna Winsted, Cynthia Copland and Jacqueline Puzzaro, who was later replaced by Judith Harris. The original Offices were located at 115 North Pennsylvania Street, Indianapolis Indiana. When that building was closed, the office was moved to 108 South Elder Avenue, Indianapolis, Indiana, which is the current address.

The original date of incorporation was chosen to place the business on a cycle that was reasonably harmonious to the greatest number of the people involved in the business. It became clear through developing the business course that the business needed to be on the same cycle as Daniel R. Hardt, the primary decision maker. It was re-incorporated on December 23, 2009, under the same name. Several of the core numbers were changed by this new date. It is set up as a C corporation because of the expansive vision of the business (22/4 integrative vision number.)

Office and Style

The current office is located in what was a separate apartment in our home. It is adequate in size for the current operation since most of the work is done by means of telephone and internet and through independent contractors, but will need to be moved as the business expands. The digits of the address reduce to 9, which is a good match to my personal numbers, but with the re-incorporation does not provide the numbers needed by the business. The space needs to be upgraded, as the 8 expression requires a greater measure of elegance and formality. Elder reduces to 8; the combined digits and street name also total 8, which lends a needed energy to the office, but brings a money conflict between the 8 and the 9.

The primary corporate color is burgundy (The word reduces to a 4 to match the 22/4 integrative vision number. It is a red Tone, which agrees with the 1 life path.) This color is used in the décor as well as on the business cards, stationery and brochures.

The structure of the office is hierarchical (19/1 life path number) with a formal structure (22/4 integrative vision number.) This business requires strong management talent (26/8 expression) with an underlying connection to people. It must be a top down structure to provide a consistent operation.

The business is motivated (16/7 soul urge) by a love for the study of numerology and researching into new levels of understanding.

People who are unfamiliar with Life Path Numerology Center, Inc, will immediately see the pioneering spirit and innovative ideas flowing from it (19/1 personality). The first impression is not a façade, but emphasizes the path the corporation is following (19/1 life path.)

Telephone Number – 317-638-9752: The business has had the same telephone number since its inception. It is too well established to change. The primary consideration is 9752 which reduces to 23/5. The 5 brings in opportunity and unexpected contacts. Since it matches the 5 founding day, it has a vibratory connection to the core. The prefix of 638 reduces to 17/8 and is a match to the expression. The combined total reduces to 4, which matches the integrative vision. The 317 area code reduces to an 11/2, which is not a direct match with any core number, but as a master number, it brings support for the 22 integrative vision. This number is appropriate for this business.

Toll free number - 800-442-2589 (Now discontinued because most clients have unlimited long distance)). The toll free number has 2589 which reduces to 24/6. 6 is the most balanced of the numbers and can work in harmony with most of the core energy. The prefix, 442 reduces to 1, a match for the life path and the personality. It reinforces the first impression. The total reduces to 7, which adds to the study and research energy of the soul urge. This number is a reasonable match.

Expansion

The corporation must prepare from the onset for major expansion (22/4 integrative vision number.) A master plan must be created in a step by step format to be sure that each added function and product is directed toward the same end.

The building blocks of this master plan are teaching, personal and business consultation, market development, professional training and product development. All these elements work together to establish a comprehensive center for the study and promotion of numerology.

The goal is to set up separate divisions for personal growth, business development and professional training, each headed up by a qualified expert. The Publishing House did not fit within the master plan, and has been phased out.

Marketing and Sales Plan

The numbers of the corporation are predominately practical and business oriented. Therefore the marketing must emphasize financial and decision making elements over service and caring. Customer service is a major part of the operation of the business, but should not be the emphasis of the marketing. Each anticipated division will have a separate marketing approach.

Business Division

- *Networking.*
- *Indy Rainbow Chamber of Commerce, Alumni Association, meetings, referrals.*
- *Free Business Seminars.*
- *90 minute seminars to reach the business community, followed by a social time for mingling and questions.*

- *Personal calls.*
- *Brochures and business cards Products to promote the business use.*
- *Business Building by the Numbers, on-line class.*
- *Daily Numeroscopes.*

Personal Growth Division

- Daily Numeroscopes subscriptions.
- Psychic fairs and community events.
- Customer Follow up.
- White papers on gaining the best use from numerology.
- Encourage repeat readings.

Professional Training Division

- Audio Class Recording.
- Video Class Recording.
- Live classes.
- Affiliate Program.

As separate divisions are established, a more detailed plan will be created for each division.

This plan is subject to revision as the business unfolds, but is the foundation plan for reaching the vision of the business.

Afterword

I encourage you to Review your business plan. There is no time limit to complete the plan, but you will want to do it while the information is still fresh in your mind. The plan does not need to follow a precise format and does not need to be perfect. If you are using the plan as a basis for your business, get started. It can be modified later based upon your experience. You now can look at your business from a different perspective. You may not fully understand some of the implications until you actually start to apply the elements.

How to Use This Material

With this book you have a basic understanding of how to apply numerology to your business. Keep the book available for reference as you put the information into practice. As with any new area of study, you do not become proficient by study alone. You learn the nuances of usage through continued application. There is a reason that an attorney is engaged in the practice of law or a doctor is engaged in the practice of medicine. To engage in the practice of numerology is likewise to apply the principles of numerology to daily use.

When working with the numbers, you must first evaluate how much detail you want to use. As with most business activities, there is an appropriate balance between spending too much time in the planning or not having the basics in place. It is possible to get so detailed that you become bogged down in trivial nuances. Determining the appropriate name and start date are the initial concerns. These factors cannot be changed without making a fresh start. If you get these elements correct, you can tweak lesser elements after you get the business going.

Limitations of the Book

This book has covered a lot of detail. You have a greater knowledge of the application of numerology in business than many numerologists. The business use is not a major part of most practices. The course is designed for your personal use. It does not qualify you to hold yourself out as a consultant without a broader background in the full gamut of numerology. This course was limited to those aspects that are pertinent to establishing a new business or tweaking an established business. A broader understanding of the numbers is necessary to gain the competence that would allow you to practice in the field.

In your business, you make decisions that affect your own business interests. Holding yourself out as a practitioner carries an additional responsibility to your clients. If your advice is inadequate, you could open yourself up to legal liability.

For those who came to this book with a solid background in numerology, the added information from this study could qualify you to proceed as a business consultant.

Further Study Opportunities

For those of you who came to this book with no other background, but are intrigued enough to want to pursue the field, further study will be necessary. I look forward to the time when a wide choice of classes and higher training will be available. The present opportunities are limited. Life Path Numerology Center helps to fill that gap by training and certifying professional numerologists. Perhaps some of you will help by becoming teachers and writers yourself.

I don't want to leave the impression that this Afterword is just a commercial advertisement, but I would be remiss if I did not provide information for those who want to pursue a career in numerology. We offer a 2 day basic class that covers the full personal profile and progressed charts. This class is open to anyone wanting to learn more about numerology, and is required for professional training. It is a live class, limited to 10 students to allow greater interaction and personal attention. This class includes some content that you will not find in any text. If you have read more than one book on numerology, you have noticed disagreements among the authors. This class guides you through the discrepancies based upon years of research and experience to give you the most accurate approach to numerology.

The material from this book will form the basis for an on-line class in applying numerology to business. This class should be available by mid-summer 2018. That format allows greater interaction, as well as a review of your business plan. It is being created on the Teachable.com platform.

If you prefer, Life Path Numerology Center provides a service to do a full work-up of your business. If you have followed the material to this point, you are aware that this work-up is time consuming and detailed. As a result, there is a corresponding cost involved, but putting your business on the proper footing will pay dividends for the life of the business. It is one of the best investments you can make toward your business success.

As the business plan for Life Path Numerology Center proceeds, we will need additional numerologists to work with us. Give me a call if you are interested in a career in numerology. Let's talk.

www.lifepathnumerology.com

Whether you took this course just to further your knowledge, or to apply it to your business or as a stepping stone toward further training, I hope that the material fulfilled your expectations and helped you along your path.

Appendix A

Numerology Calculation Sheet

Birth Date _____ _____ _____   Birth Day _____

Reduced _____ _____ _____   Life Path _____

Letter Conversion Table

1	2	3	4	5	6	7	8	9
A	B	C	D	E	F	G	H	I
J	K	L	M	N	O	P	Q	R
S	T	U	V	W	X	Y	Z	

Integrative Vision _____

Personal Year _____

Full Birth Name On Line 3 (complete as shown on birth certificate)

                                                                                             Soul Urge

1 _____ _____ _____   _____

2 _____ _____ _____

3 _____ _____ _____

4 _____ _____ _____

                                                                                             Personality

5 _____ _____ _____   _____

                                                                                             Expression

6 _____ _____ _____   _____

Intensification Table   **Key to the meaning of numbers**

1 (3)
2 (1)
3 (1-2)
4 (1)
5 (3-5)
6 (1-2)
7 (0-1)
8 (1)
9 (1-2)

1. Independence, Attainment
2. Co-operation, Tact, Diplomacy
3. Expressiveness, Verbal Skills
4. System, Organization, Hard Work
5. Change, Constructive Freedom
6. Responsibility, Love, Creativity
7. Analysis, Understanding
8. Material Satisfaction
9. Selfless Humanitarian
11. Master Illuminator
22. Master Builder
33. Master Teacher

Growth Number _____

Main Challenge _____

Maturity Number _____

Balance Number _____

Subconscious Response _____

Rational Thought _____

Universal Year _____

Life Path Numerology Center.   www.lifepathnumerology.com.
Daniel R. Hardt, J.D., Instructor and Reader mailto:dhardt@lifepathnum.com

Numerology Calculation Sheet

Birth Date _MAY 30 1940_   Birth Day _(30) 3_

Reduced _5_ _3_ _14/5_   Life Path _13/4_

Letter Conversion Table

1	2	3	4	5	6	7	8	9
A	B	C	D	E	F	G	H	I
J	K	L	M	N	O	P	Q	R
S	T	U	V	W	X	Y	Z	

Integrative Vision _(18) 9_

Personal Year _(10) 1_
For 2018

Full Birth Name On Line 3 (complete as shown on birth certificate)

1. _(15) 6_   _(20) 2_   _1_   _9_ Soul Urge
2. _1 95_   _59 6_   _1_
3. _DANIEL_   _REINHOLD_   _HARDT_
4. _4 5 3_   _9 58 34_   _8 942_
5. _(12) 3_   _(29) 11/2_ _(23) 5_   _19/1_ Personality
6. _(27) 9_   _(49) 13/4_ _(24) 6_   _19/1_ Expression

Intensification Table

1 (3)
2 (1)
3 (1-2)
4 (1)
5 (3-5)
6 (1-2)
7 (0-1)
8 (1)
9 (1-2)

Key to the meaning of numbers

1. Independence, Attainment
2. Co-operation, Tact, Diplomacy
3. Expressiveness, Verbal Skills
4. System, Organization, Hard Work
5. Change, Constructive Freedom
6. Responsibility, Love, Creativity
7. Analysis, Understanding
8. Material Satisfaction
9. Selfless Humanitarian
11. Master Illuminator
22. Master Builder
33. Master Teacher

Growth Number _____

Main Challenge _____

Maturity Number _____

Balance Number _____

Subconscious Response _____

Rational Thought _____

Universal Year _(2018) 11/2_

Life Path Numerology Center.   www.lifepathnumerology.com.
Daniel R. Hardt, J.D., Instructor and Reader mailto:dhardt@lifepathnum.com

Appendix B
General Characteristics of the Numbers

Learning the general characteristics of the numbers is the heart of the study. The calculations and setting up the chart are relatively simple. Just follow the recipe. Knowing the meaning of the numbers allows you to compare and contrast each segment of the chart to gain the full picture.

1
Lesson: Learn to be independent, to stand upon your own two feet without leaning on or depending upon others. Then use that independence to accomplish great things based upon your own ideas.
Traits: A born leader, erratic, innovative business ideas. Should be own boss or in business for himself. A pioneer, strong personality, not easily intimidated. Uses information for specific purpose. Can be dominating and egotistical. A risk taker with much drive and determination. Willing to try new approaches. Honest, loyal and reliable. A starter, not a finisher. Dislikes routine.

2
Lesson: Learn cooperation, tact and diplomacy in group situations
Traits: Prefers to work with others, good in partnerships. Not an initiator. Prefers to follow through on ideas of others. Refined, sensitive, passionate lover, unpretentious, willing to stay in the background. Warm and affectionate with a need to be cuddled and appreciated. A perfectionist who is easily hurt by criticism. Artistic with an eye for beauty. Seeks harmony. Persuades rather than dominates. Holds on to everything. Worries about details and the opinions of others. Good negotiator or counselor. Has healing capabilities. Shy and compliant, supportive, modest. Traditional, maybe even a bit old-fashioned.

3
Lesson: Learn to Express the Joy in Living
Traits: Very social, needs an audience. Has a facility with written and spoken words. Quick witted, charismatic and charming. Happy, friendly, outgoing. Loves a good time. Playful, extroverted but with good emotional and mental balance. Lacks discipline, disorganized, irresponsible, inspiring, and charming, with a gift of gab. Generous and happy-go-lucky. Life of the party, popular, center of attention. Has a dramatic flair. Flamboyant and fashionable.

Covers over feelings with laughter and jokes. Original, intuitive, creative. Emotional, sometimes to the point of melodrama. Good sense of harmony. Superficial approach and pursuit of the trivial can lead to loneliness even in a crowd.

4
Lesson: Learn to put system and organization into work and to pay attention to details
Traits: Practical, down-to-earth. Quick to judge, but with an underlying compassion for people. Reliable, methodical, systematic. Responsible, stable, secure. Conservative, not creative, detailed and too serious. Trustworthy, moralistic, honest. Has strong likes and dislikes. A survivor. Good provider. Family is important. Shrewd, often untactful, narrowly focused. Loves nature and manual work. Can be dull, frugal, dominating and demanding

5
Lesson: Learn to use freedom constructively
Traits: Wants to try everything. Can be overindulgent. True free spirit with an eclectic mind. Learns best by experience. Fresh ideas and a quick tongue. Likes the unusual. Flows with life, needs change and excitement. Creative, dynamic, alive. Can do almost anything, and most things very well. Scatters energies with too many activities. Quickly bored and on to a new interest. Nervous energy, socially oriented, a promoter, unconventional. Wants to save the world and may promise more than can be delivered. Not easily fooled. Not prejudiced. Loves the exotic and unusual. Resourceful and communicative.

6
Lesson: Learn the deep satisfaction of handling responsibility appropriately
Traits: The cosmic parent. Often neglects own needs for others, but can interfere by imposing his ideas upon others. Counselor and healer. Good listener. The consummate caregiver. Drawn to those who are in need or too weak to care for themselves. Understanding, patient, warm. A passionate lover, centered upon home and family. Hospitable, protective, not a good judge of character. Often used by others. Well-balanced, generous, kind, dutiful, just and honest. Intuitive and spiritual. Good teacher, socially conscious, emotional but disciplined. A paradox of emotions. Responsible and trustworthy. Domestic, artistic. Good sense of balance and harmony. Good taste.

7
Lesson: To know yourself
Traits: Different, scholarly, dignified, inhibited. Needs time alone to contemplate and to study. Suppresses emotions behind a shield. Analytical mind, keen intuition. Wants to know everything. Does not judge by surface appearances. Drawn to scientific, technical or metaphysical pursuits. Charming and attractive. Can be life of the party, but tells little about himself. Relies upon own judgment. Not particularly trusting. Intelligent, serious, wise and understanding. May be distant, aloof and impersonal, but really desires closeness. Not a risk taker, not impulsive. Distrusts emotions in self and in others. Spiritual and religious. Unusual insights, unique solutions.

8
Lesson: learn the satisfactions of the physical world and the appropriate use of power balanced by a spiritual understanding
Traits: Natural leader, goal oriented. Quality conscious. Needs to make a good impression. Wants the finest in life and will do whatever is necessary to get it. Balances ideals with the hard realities. Often severely tested, but rebounds with courage and tenacity. Realistic, direct and outspoken. Quick learner, not likely to repeat mistakes. Money centered. Proud of family, usually many children. Can achieve greatness, but often after many setbacks. Impressive personality, which may be intimidating. Ambitious, impervious and controlling. Can delegate duties, but a demanding leader.

9
Lesson: Learn the satisfaction of giving without thought of return
Traits: Humanitarian, philanthropic. Wants to change the world. Creative and artistic. A perfectionist who is often disappointed when ideals aren't met. Easily taken advantage of. Moody or arrogant. Great compassion for mankind. Works well with groups. Attracts money mysteriously and unexpectedly. Charming, well-liked. charismatic, intuitive, dramatic, emotional. Expressive of feelings. Fascinated with people. Not many are neutral to a 9, they are either attracted or repulsed. Not a good judge of character. Often misreads others.

Master Numbers

11
Lesson: On a mission to bring illumination and enlightenment to the world.
Traits: Incorporates the traits of the 2 and raises them to a higher vibration. Inspiring, wise, intuitive, psychic. A channel of energy and the higher powers. Inventive, ambitious. A powerful presence. Romantic, idealistic. Selective of friends, but yet attracts the wrong people. Impractical and unrealistic. Has an eye for beauty, harmony, balance and rhythm. Perceptive. Good counselor, advisor, teacher. Not businesslike. A thinker, not a doer. Extremely sensitive, may be unstable. Lacks self-confidence. Multifaceted, visionary. May lack direction.

22
Lesson: Master the combination of the highest ideals with the largest material goals
Traits: Incorporates the traits of the 4 and raises them to a higher vibration. Powerful with ultimate success potential. Power is based upon ideals. Great ambition, great strength, good intuition. Enormous potential, but may lack self-confidence for fulfillment. Efficient, methodical, practical visionary. Wants to change history. A leader. Good common sense. Results oriented and dependable. Managerial, persistent. Hates pretension. Not prejudiced. Influential, noticed. Can be eccentric or arrogant. Intuitively knows what will work.

33
Lesson: Hold the master vibration to bless those in need through conscious focus
Traits: Incorporates the traits of the 6 and raises them to a higher vibration. The master teacher - teacher of teachers. Kind and generous. Concerned for the welfare of the world. Christ-like ideals. Expanded consciousness. Outgoing and giving. Keen sense of duty and

justice. A reformer. Creative manifestation and expansion. Philanthropic. Leads by example. Highly dedicated. Brings light to the world.

Karmic Numbers
13/4 Challenge: to learn to work in a step-by-step manner from an organized plan, and not to quit just as the goal is in sight. Tends to work with blinders on. Doesn't always see what is really being accomplished. Will do the job his way, even if it makes the job harder.
14/5 Challenge: tempted by the physical pleasures. Goes to excess in food, sex, drugs and alcohol if not curbed by will-power.
16/7 Challenge: Relationships are difficult. Unwilling to open up to a partner. Buries feelings. Puts up a shield to prevent closeness.
19/1 Challenge: Forgets that his actions impact others. Oblivious to any but self interests.

Appendix C
Aspects Chart

H = Harmonious   D = Discordant   M = Mixed
Use the reduced number for master numbers.

1

1-2	D	1 is active, an initiator	2 is passive, sensitive, emotional	
1-3	M	1 is a doer	3 is a talker	Both are creative
1-4	H	1 is an innovator	4 is a hard worker	Both are business oriented
1-5	M	1 is focused	5 is scattered, easily bored	Both seek new approaches
1-6	M	1 is independent	6 nurturing, caring, connected to people	Both have a business aspect
1-7	D	1 acts creatively	7 is deep thinking, analytical,	Both are intuitive- and independent
1-8	H	1 is a leader	8 is a manager	Both work from a practical base
1-9	D	1 works from logic	9 is emotional, idealistic	

2

2-1	D	2 is passive, sensitive, emotional	1 is active, an initiator	
2-3	D	2 is withdrawn	3 is social	
2-4	M	2 invites confidences	4 focuses on own work	Both are detail oriented
2-5	D	2 is unobtrusive	5 is flamboyant	
2-6	H	2 is sensitive to balance, color	6 is a performer, care-giver, good taste	Both are responsible, Sensitive to people
2-7	D	2 is sensitive, emotional	7 is aloof, shielded	

| 2-8 | M | 2 is a follower | 8 is a manager | Both have business acumen |
| 2-9 | H | 2 is detailed | 9 is a perfectionist | Both are creative and artistic |

3

3-1	M	3 is a talker	1 is a doer	Both are creative
3-2	D	3 is social	2 is withdrawn	
3-4	D	3 is a spendthrift	4 is frugal	
3-5	H	3 has persuasive skill with words	5 is a risk taker	Both are sales people
3-6	H	3 is creative	6 is a performer, care giver	Both connect with people
3-7	D	3 is gregarious	7 is withdrawn	
3-8	D	3 is scattered	8 is focused	
3-9	H			Both are creative, reach out to people

4

4-1	H	4 is a hard worker	1 is an innovator	Both are business oriented
4-2	M	4 is practical	2 is emotional	Both pay attention to detail
4-3	D	4 is stoic, frugal	3 is loquacious, spendthrift	
4-5	D	4 is focused	5 is scattered	
4-6	M	4 is a provider	6 is nurturing	Both have business acumen
4-7	D	4 is physical, practical	7 is mental, analytical	
4-8	H	4 is persistent	8 is in control	Both are concerned with finances
4-9	D	4 is practical, logical	9 is emotional, idealistic	

5

5=1	M	5 wants the cutting edge	1 has innovative ideas	Both bring a fresh approach
5-2	D	5 is easily bored	2 is diligent in follow through	
5-3	H	5 is active, risk taking	3 is a persuasive talker	Both are quick witted
5-4	D	5 is scattered, easily bored	4 is a diligent worker	
5-6	D	5 is out and about	6 is considerate, nurturing	
5-7	D	5 is Active, always busy	7 is introspective, analytical	

5-8	D	5 can be irresponsible	8 is in control	
5-9	D	5 is unemotional	9 is emotional	

6

6-1	M	6 is nurturing, and care giving	1 is independent	Both are business oriented
6-2	H	6 needs all in good taste	2 sensitive to environs	Both connect with family and friends
6-3	H	6 has performing talent	3 has skill with spoken or written words	Both can be emotional
6-4	M	6 has business skill	4 is a diligent worker	Both are concerned for family
6-5	D	6 is balanced in logic and feelings	5 discounts emotion	
6-7	D	6 reaches out to people	7 puts up a shield	
6-8	H	6 has a balanced business skill	8 is the ultimate manager	
6-9	H	6 is a care giver	9 desires to improve society	Both are people oriented

7

7-1	D	7 is a researcher	1 is an active innovator	
7-2	D	7 buries emotion	2 works from an emotional base	
7-3	D	7 is introspective	3 is outgoing	
7-4	D	7 is a thinker	4 is a doer	Both are practical
7-5	D	7 is withdrawn	5 wants to do everything	
7-6	D	7 is unaffected by surroundings	6 is aware of good taste	
7-8	D	7 knows money will be there as needed	8 is ambitious for money	
7-9	M	7 ponders and evaluates	9 promotes societal upgrades	Both are intuitive

8

8-1	H	8 controls others	1 does his own business	
8-2	M	8 is commanding	2 negotiates	Both are diligent
8-3	D	8 is responsible	3 is scattered	
8-4	H	8 is a leader	4 is an independent worker	Both are logical, unemotional
8-5	D	8 is a planner	5 goes off on a whim	

8-6	H	8 manages and delegates	6 can lead or follow	Both have business acumen
8-7	D	8 is always aware of money	7 does not worry about money	
8-9	D	8 needs to control the outcome	9 follows an ideal	

9

9-1	D	9 is emotional	1 is practical	
9-2	H	9 is a perfectionist	2 takes care of details	Both are emotional
9-3	H	9 reaches out to others	3 is a communicator	Both strive for improvement
9-4	D	9 is emotional	4 is logical	
9-5	D	9 is visionary	5 acts upon impulse	
9-6	H	9 wants to improve society	6 emphasized home and family	Both are creative, artistic
9-7	M	9 is Reaches out to others	7 is aloof	Both are intuitive, psychic
9-8	D	9 is generous, forgiving	8 is all business	

www.ingramcontent.com/pod-product-compliance
Ingram Content Group UK Ltd.
Pitfield, Milton Keynes, MK11 3LW, UK
UKHW050414240426
12048UKWH00020B/1505